Managing Accounting Systems & People

Combined text

NVQ Accounting Unit 10
AAT Diploma Pathway Unit 10

Michael Fardon

osborne
BOOKS

Published by Osborne Books Limited
Unit 1B Everoak Estate
Bromyard Road
Worcester WR2 5HP
Tel 01905 748071
Email books@osbornebooks.co.uk
Website www.osbornebooks.co.uk

Design by Richard Holt
Cover image from Getty Images

Printed by CPI Antony Rowe Limited, Chippenham.

British Library Cataloguing in Publication Data
A catalogue record for this book is available from the British Library

ISBN 978 1872962 429

Contents

Acknowledgements

The author wishes to thank the following for their help with the production of the book: Ruth Brown, Rosemarie Griffiths and Claire McCarthy. The author is also grateful to Bryn Griffiths and Roger Petheram of Worcester College of Technology for reading the text and making useful suggestions and to John Prokopiw for providing material on the principles of management and management theory. Special thanks must go to Clare Eccleston and Ann Fontbin of Hereford College of Technology for reading the text, and contributing practical ideas and advice about the delivery of Unit 10. The publisher is particularly grateful to those students who have kindly given permission for the use and adaptation of original Project material which appears in this text.

Lastly, the publisher is indebted to the Association of Accounting Technicians for permission for the reproduction of extracts from the Accounting Standards and the sample Case Study, Delmar Electronics Limited.

Author

Michael Fardon has extensive teaching experience of a wide range of banking, business and accountancy courses at Worcester College of Technology. Earlier in his career he worked in a major international bank. He now specialises in writing business and financial texts and is General Editor at Osborne Books. He is also an educational consultant and has worked extensively in the areas of vocational business curriculum development.

Preface

Managing Accounting Systems & People has been written to cover the requirements of NVQ and AAT Diploma Pathway Unit 10 'Managing Systems & People in the Accounting Environment'.

Managing Accounting Systems & People is designed as a practical guide to what can be a challenging Unit which involves the writing of a four thousand word Project.

The subject of the Project is the assessment of an accounting system and its management, leading to recommendations for change and improvement. This in turn is followed by an assessment of the success of that change. The Project is ideally based on a real workplace accounting system, but may also be written as part of an AAT simulation based on a Case Study.

Managing Accounting Systems & People is divided into five sections:

1   an introduction to what is required in the Project

2   a guide to planning and writing the Project, introducing the Performance Criteria that will have to be covered

3   an explanation of the theory behind the Project, together with questions which can produce evidence for the underlying Knowledge & Understanding

4   examples of student reports

5   a sample AAT Case Study (but not a simulation) providing an insight into the areas of an accounting system, typical of the subject matter examined in a Unit 10 Project

Blood and tears are reputed to have been shed in the writing of Unit 10 Projects, but it is hoped that this practical guide will help to reduce the stresses and strains sometimes associated with the Unit.

Michael Fardon

Support available

In addition to the traditional forms of support provided by the college assessor and the workplace mentor, students should find useful the following websites listed below.

The details provided here were correct at the time of writing but they may be subject to change and update. Many websites have a search facility, so if the required material is not immediately apparent, the keying in of significant terms such as 'fraud' can reveal what is needed.

www.aat.co.uk	The AAT website contains a wealth of material and resources to assist students with the Project. Downloadable resources include Unit 10 Project Guidance.
	There is also a lively Student Discussion Forum which often features comments on the difficulties of Project writing.
www.icaew.co.uk	The Institute of Chartered Accountants in England and Wales has a useful report – 'Fighting Fraud' available for download.
www.sfo.gov.uk	The Serious Fraud Office website has a wealth of material relating to fraud.
www.hm-treasury.gov.uk.	The Treasury Fraud reports, which cover public sector fraud, make interesting reading, and are downloadable.
www.google.co.uk	This is one of the best search engines on the net. Type in a key word for a UK search to access a wide (and sometimes unexpected) range of material.

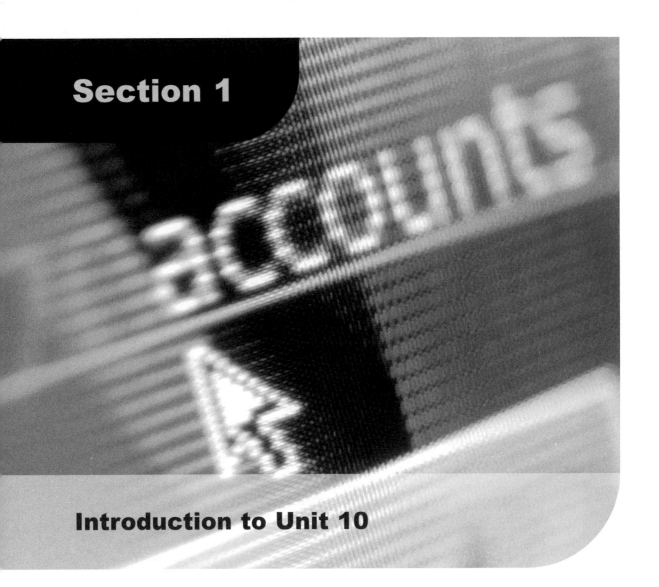

Section 1

Introduction to Unit 10

1 Introduction to the Unit

this chapter covers . . .

The aim of this chapter is to summarise what you will be expected to do to provide the assessment evidence – including the 'Project' – required by Unit 10 'Managing Systems and People in the Accounting Environment'.

The chapter includes:

- *an overview of the Project writing process and the people it will involve*

- *the need to choose a workplace to form the context of the Project*

- *the way in which this textbook is structured and how it 'works'*

- *the possibility of using an AAT Simulation when a workplace is not available*

- *an explanation of how the Project fits in with your studies*

PERFORMANCE CRITERIA COVERED

Unit 10:
MANAGING SYSTEMS AND PEOPLE IN THE ACCOUNTING ENVIRONMENT

Element 10.1   Manage people within the accounting environment

Element 10.2   Identify opportunities for improving the effectiveness of an accounting system

This chapter by virtue of its introductory nature does not specifically cover the performance criteria requirements or the underlying Knowledge and Understanding. These will be covered in full in later chapters.

UNIT 10 REQUIREMENTS

A summary of the requirements for Unit 10 is set out in the Unit Commentary published by AAT. The Unit has two separate Elements, for which you have to provide evidence:

Element 10.1   Manage people within the accounting environment

Element 10.2   Identify opportunities for improving the effectiveness of an accounting system

The Unit Commentary reads as follows . . .

> This unit is about your role as a manager in the accounting environment, whether you are a line manager or are managing a particular function or Project.
>
> The first element requires you to show that you co-ordinate work activities effectively within the accounting environment. This includes setting realistic objectives, targets and deadlines and managing people in such a way that these can be met. You also need to show that you prepare contingency plans to cover a variety of problems that can reduce the likelihood of meeting objectives, targets and deadlines.
>
> The second element is about identifying weaknesses in an accounting system and making recommendations to rectify these. This involves identifying potential for misuse of a system, whether this is accidental (errors) or deliberate (fraud). You are also required to update the system, for example to comply with legislative requirements, and to check that the output is correct after the system has been updated.

In short, in an ideal world . . .

* the **first element** requires you to know about managing an accounting office (or part of it) and knowing what to do when things go wrong

* the **second element** requires you to examine this accounting system, suggest how the system and its management can be improved and check that all is running well after the improvements have been made

But you probably do not live in an ideal world. It may be that you are a manager in an accounting environment, but it is statistically more likely that you are not, in which case you may well be asking yourself how this Unit relates to your situation and how on earth you are going to be able to provide the necessary evidence.

It is our aim in this book to give you guidance so that you will be able to produce this evidence, even if you are not a manager, not working in an accounting environment and maybe not even working at all.

The evidence will prove your competence in a variety of performance criteria and show that you have an acceptable level of knowledge and understanding for Unit 10. The evidence will take the form of:

- a 3,000-4,000 word Report (the 'Project') analysing an accounting system, identifying weaknesses, recommending solutions and, where possible, assessing the success of the recommendations you have made

- answers to written or oral questions on areas covered by the Unit requirements but not included in the evidence produced by your Report

THE 'PROJECT'

As you will have gathered, the basis of your assessment is a 4,000 word Report, often referred to as 'The Project'. It is our aim in this book to make the writing of this Project as smooth and painless as possible. Once you have got over the initial barrier of staring at a blank piece of paper or a blank screen and wondering what you are going to write about, the process should be relatively straightforward. In most cases you will have people to help you both at your training centre and also at your workplace, and you also have this text to fill in the gaps in your knowledge and understanding.

The diagram on the opposite page shows you the processes that you will go through to successfully produce your evidence – to complete the Project and answer any extra questioning that is required. Please study it carefully and then read on. The notes that follow explain the diagram – literally from top to bottom.

finding a 'workplace'

One of the most difficult parts of writing the Unit 10 Project is making initial decisions. You will have to decide:

- what organisation (if any) you are going to use as a basis for your Project
- what aspect of that organisation you are going to write about

If you are an accounts manager, life is made easy for you, but if you are currently not working and are studying to get a qualification to enable you to work, the situation is more complex. The next chapter 'What are you going to write about?' covers this area in detail, but at this stage you should be aware that if you do not work in an accounting environment or at all, you can choose a workplace to study (possibly through a friend or family) or an organisation such as a club which has an accounting function.

If none of these options is open to you, there are AAT Simulations which can be used as a basis for your Project, but these should be used only as a last resort.

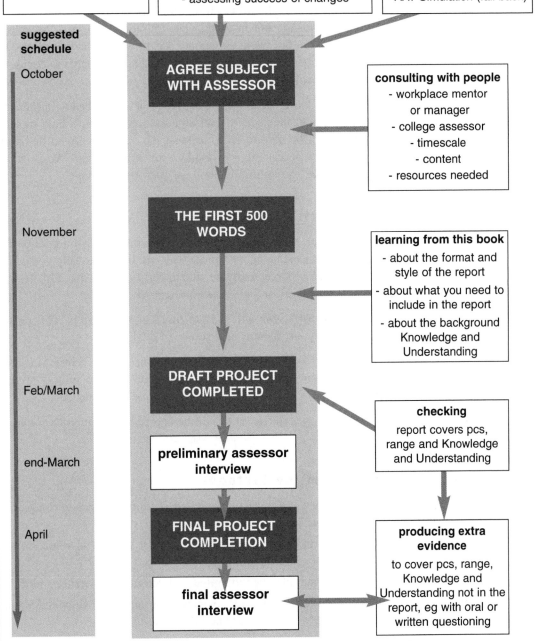

suggested Unit 10 assessment plan

choosing workplace
or other organisation
to assess
as the basis of the report

choosing subject area
within the accounting system
- evaluating system and use of people
- improving system and use of people
- assessing success of changes

using experience
- own management
experience, or
- observing managers, or,
- AAT Simulation (fall back)

suggested schedule

October

November

Feb/March

end-March

April

AGREE SUBJECT WITH ASSESSOR

THE FIRST 500 WORDS

DRAFT PROJECT COMPLETED

preliminary assessor interview

FINAL PROJECT COMPLETION

final assessor interview

consulting with people
- workplace mentor
or manager
- college assessor
- timescale
- content
- resources needed

learning from this book
- about the format and
style of the report
- about what you need to
include in the report
- about the background
Knowledge and
Understanding

checking
report covers pcs,
range and Knowledge
and Understanding

producing extra evidence
to cover pcs, range,
Knowledge and
Understanding not in the
report, eg with oral or
written questioning

choosing a subject

The next choice is the subject of your Project. There is further guidance on this in the next chapter. In a nutshell, you will need to find an area in an accounting environment – eg payroll processing, paying suppliers, cash handling, job costing – which could be improved so that its processes become more efficient and less open to error and to fraud.

If you are in work, this should be straightforward, as you will have time to look around. If you are not in work, your training centre may be able to arrange for you to do work experience or to work shadow. Time for investigation will be more limited here, but you should be able to decide on a subject for the Project.

If you are not in work, or if work experience or work shadowing are not possible, you should then identify an organisation such as a club or local charity which will be able to help, or twist the arm of a friend or family member who has access to a workplace or organisation. An area for investigation in the accounting function can then be identified.

consulting with other people

It is important that, if you are in employment, you establish a relationship with a mentor (advisor) in the workplace who will be able to help you gather evidence and who will eventually be able to certify your work. This mentor might be a line manager or a more senior manager.

If you are not in work, you will have to find someone who is. This person will then become your 'mentor' and source of evidence.

You will also need to identify your assessor at your training centre. He or she should provide you with support, discussing with you the subject of your Project and monitoring its progress as you compile the evidence.

Whatever subject you choose, it should be agreed both with your employer or contact and also your assessor (eg your college tutor).

learning from the textbook

Unit 10 is often seen as a 'difficult' Unit and a stumbling block to completing your qualifications. This is understandable:

- a Project has to be written, with no subject given and often limited opportunity for gathering evidence
- the Project format may be unfamiliar and you may get 'writer's block'
- you are required to provide evidence of areas of Knowledge and Understanding to which it may be difficult to relate

It is the aim of the textbook to help you in all these areas by:

- explaining what is required in the Project

- explaining the format of a Project

- providing the necessary Knowledge and Understanding – eg an outline of the types of fraud, management theories

- providing questions which can be used to produce evidence for the Knowledge and Understanding requirements

- providing examples of actual Reports

It is therefore worth spending time to appreciate how the textbook is structured, so that you can make the most of its resources.

structure of this textbook

This textbook is divided into five separate sections:

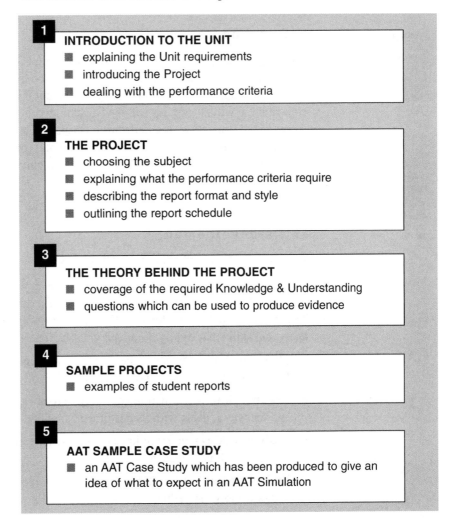

1

INTRODUCTION TO THE UNIT
- explaining the Unit requirements
- introducing the Project
- dealing with the performance criteria

2

THE PROJECT
- choosing the subject
- explaining what the performance criteria require
- describing the report format and style
- outlining the report schedule

3

THE THEORY BEHIND THE PROJECT
- coverage of the required Knowledge & Understanding
- questions which can be used to produce evidence

4

SAMPLE PROJECTS
- examples of student reports

5

AAT SAMPLE CASE STUDY
- an AAT Case Study which has been produced to give an idea of what to expect in an AAT Simulation

In order to make the most of the textbook, you should:

- start by reading Section 1, which introduces the Unit, and think about what workplace or other scenario you are going to choose which will form the basis of your Project

- study Section 2 'The Project' which will explain about the format of the Project, help you to choose the subject to be covered and make sure that you understand the performance criteria that have to be tackled

- study Section 3 'The Theory behind the Project' which will ensure that you cover all the Knowledge and Understanding requirements

- refer to Section 4 'Sample Reports' which includes examples of a variety of student projects

- refer to Section 5 'AAT Sample Case Study' if you expect to use an AAT Simulation (but note that this is not to be used as a Simulation)

time schedule

The diagram on page 5 suggests a time schedule (October to April) for the writing and the assessment of the Project – see the time line on the left-hand side of the diagram. This is only a suggestion, but it has been drawn up after consultation with a number of AAT teaching centres. We will cover the stages in the Project writing in detail in Chapter 3, but the important point to note here is that the writing and assessment process should ideally be completed by the end of April so that there is plenty of time for preparation for the June exams.

skills development

A question often asked about Unit 10 is 'why?'

One of the reasons for the inclusion of the Project writing exercise is that it develops the type of **skills** that are expected of a qualification of this level. These skills will complement the 'number-crunching' and technical analytical skills that rightly dominate your studies. They include:

- **planning skills** – planning the research, writing and presentation of the Project, using time and other resources efficiently

- **research skills** – you will have to research an organisation, its products, and the way it deals with its customers, suppliers and competitors

- **analytical skills** – you will have to analyse an accounting system and the way in which it is managed

- **Project writing** – you will have to present a report in an accepted format and develop your written communication skills

- **oral communication** – you will be interviewed and questioned a number of times on your Project in its various stages of compilation by your assessor and may also discuss the Project and its recommendations with your workplace mentor

On completion of the Project you should ideally be in a position where you have made a material difference to the way in which an accounting system operates and its management functions. Even if you have adopted the AAT Simulation method of generating evidence you will still have developed the skills mentioned above.

PRODUCING THE EVIDENCE

performance criteria

The Project for Unit 10 involves two **elements**:

Element 10.1   Manage people within the accounting environment

Element 10.2   Identify opportunities for improving the effectiveness of an accounting system

Coverage of the **performance criteria** is not as daunting as you might think. Set out below are some of the criteria to be covered:

	Performance criteria - in order to perform this element successfully you need to			
A	Plan work activities to make the optimum use of resources and to ensure that work is completed within agreed timescales			
B	Review the competence of individuals undertaking work activities and arrange the necessary training			
C	Prepare, in collaboration with management, **contingency plans** to meet possible emergencies			

Do not be put off by the performance criteria which state requirements such as 'Review the competence of individuals undertaking work activities and arrange the necessary training.' This relates to the possibility that you are a manager in an accounting office. It does not matter if you are a not a manager in an accounting office or even if you are not working in an accounting office. In fact, it does not matter if you are not working. It is quite acceptable for assessment purposes if you discuss what you would do if you were placed in these situations.

There is a full list of the performance criteria on pages 20 to 26.

knowledge and understanding – the theory

The Unit specifications require an understanding of the Knowledge & Understanding which underpin the writing of the Project. For example, as shown below, you will need to gain a basic knowledge of the theories and principles of management:

	Knowledge and understanding - to perform this unit effectively you will need to know and understand:			
10	Principles of supervision and delegation (Element 10.1)			
11	Principles of fostering effective working relationships, building teams and motivating staff (Element 10.1)			

Areas of knowledge and understanding such as these are covered in Section 3 of this book 'The Theory behind the Project', which provides the knowledge that you will need.

AAT SIMULATIONS

As mentioned earlier, AAT produces Case Study Simulations which can be used as a basis for your Project, but these should be resorted to only if you cannot find a suitable workplace scenario.

The same principles for the production of evidence outlined above should be used with a Simulation. You should treat the Case Study in the Simulation as you would any workplace and discuss the progress of your Project with your assessor in exactly the same way. An AAT sample Case Study is reproduced on pages 123-150 of this text.

There are no formal activities at the end of this chapter. Instead there is guidance about what stage you should have reached before moving on to the next chapter.

Student Guidance

guidance notes

1   Decide on the workplace you will use as a basis for your Project.

     This should be chosen in the following order of priority

     (a)   your own workplace, if you have one

     (b)   a workplace you will be going to as part of a work placement scheme or work shadowing

     (c)   a workplace to which you can gain access through a friend or member of the family

     (d)   a club or an association to which you belong, which has an accounting system

     (e)   an AAT Simulation

2   If you have chosen from options (a) to (d) above, identify someone as a work 'mentor' who can help and advise you as you write the Project. This person might be your boss, but it could also be another employee who is in a position of responsibility who will be able to help and guide you with your Project writing.

3   Make a short-list of possible areas which you could make the subject of your report, ie parts of the accounting system which you think you can improve in some way by changing the method of management and operation. Use the next page to write down ideas if you wish. It is left blank for your ideas.

4   If you have chosen from options (a) to (d) in Note 1, start to collect information about the organisation, eg its history, products, customers, organisational structure. Make sure that the information you have collected is not confidential and that you have permission to use it in your Project should you want to.

The next section 'The Project' gives practical guidance on

•   *choosing what to write about*

•   *the format of the Project*

•   *coverage of the performance criteria*

•   *drawing up a schedule and targets for completion of the various parts of the Project*

inspiration page

Section 2

The Project

This Section contains two chapters:

This Section gives practical advice and guidance about

- ■ choosing a subject area for the Project and discussing it with your assessor and workplace mentor

- ■ explaining the need to incorporate the evidence required by the performance criteria

- ■ the format and style of the Project report

- ■ planning and timetabling the Project

- ■ the responsibilities of the student, the assessor and the workplace mentor or manager

After reading the last chapter you should have identified the workplace (or workplace scenario) that you are going to use as a basis for your Project.

This chapter provides guidance for the next major decision that you will have to make – the subject of your Project. This will involve:

- *identifying areas of the accounting system which may need improving*

- *discussing the options with your workplace mentor and establishing whether the issue of confidentiality will restrict you*

- *discussing the chosen subject with your assessor (eg college tutor) and getting approval*

When you have agreed the subject matter and cleared the confidentiality aspect with your workplace you will then be in a position to prepare an outline plan of the Project.

At this point you will need to be aware of the performance criteria for which you need to provide evidence as you will eventually need to map them against your Project content. This chapter explains what is needed for each of the performance criteria.

PERFORMANCE CRITERIA COVERED

unit 10:
MANAGING SYSTEMS AND PEOPLE IN THE ACCOUNTING ENVIRONMENT

Element 10.1   Manage people within the accounting environment

Element 10.2   Identify opportunities for improving the effectiveness of an accounting system

This chapter explains the performance criteria requirements for these two Elements on pages 20 to 26 and makes suggestions about how the Project can be used to provide evidence.

The Knowledge and Understanding requirements for the two Elements will be covered in Chapters 4, 5 and 6 (pages 50 to 84).

OBJECTIVES OF THE PROJECT

We will first look at the **objectives** of the Project, in other words, what you will expect to have achieved by the time you have completed your report. These are set out in the two elements of Unit 10. When you are familiar with these objectives you will then be in a better position to be able to plan what you are going to write about.

It is important to appreciate that Elements 10.1 and 10.2 are not consecutive, but run side-by-side:

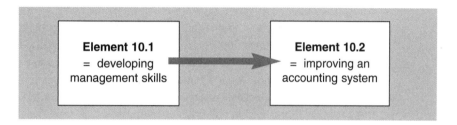

element 10.1 = developing management skills

The first of the two elements in Unit 10 requires you to

> 'co-ordinate work activities effectively within the accounting environment. This includes setting realistic objectives, targets and deadlines and managing people in such a way that these can be met. You also need to show that you prepare contingency plans to cover a variety of problems that can reduce the likelihood of meeting objectives, targets and deadlines.'

As mentioned in the last chapter, this may seem an unrealistic target when you may not be in a management position or may not be working at all. What is required of you when presenting your Project is that you have **an appreciation of the issues facing managers** in an accounting environment. In your Project you will be expected to deal with 'what if' questions such as:

'**what if** a target or deadline is not met?'

'**what** would you do about it **if** you were in a position of responsibility?'

In other words you will need to show an understanding of management issues and be able to suggest workable solutions when targets are not met. You will also need to know how to deal with people who find it difficult to work together to achieve targets and deadlines.

This analysis of **management skills** relates to the part of your Project where you have already identified a weakness in the accounting system, or an area which could be changed according to your recommendations. In other words, you first have to suggest a solution to a problem in the accounting system (Element 10.2) and then use management skills to plan the changes and sort it all out, dealing with possible disruptions to the plan along the way (Element 10.1).

element 10.2 = improving an accounting system

The second element is where you start. You first have to find an accounting workplace – real, second-hand or imaginary (an AAT Simulation) and then identify an area which could be improved. The AAT specification states that this element

> 'is about identifying weaknesses in an accounting system and making recommendations to rectify these. This involves identifying potential for misuse of a system, whether this is accidental (errors) or deliberate (fraud). You are also required to update the system, for example to comply with legislative requirements, and to check that the output is correct after the system has been updated.'

The weakness in the system can relate to suspect procedures which could cause **errors** to be made (eg inefficient recording of money received by a business) or, in a worse case, **fraud** (eg employees dipping their hand in the till when they know that the theft may not be picked up).

It is your task to recommend ways of rectifying the problem you have identified, put your recommendations into action and then check that the new system is running satisfactorily and according to plan.

You may rightly say that the reality gap seems to be widening here. In view of your personal circumstances, can this really happen? AAT acknowledges that this may not be the case and is normally happy to accept Projects based on **proposed** recommendations and **proposed** solutions to problems in implementation that **could** occur.

It is in these circumstances that it is important to build up good relationships with both your workplace mentor and your training assessor. They will be able to talk you through both the planning and the writing of the Project.

CHOOSING THE SUBJECT

the overview

An 'accounting system' is a very general term, and depending on the size of the organisation involved, can be used to describe the work carried out by a few people or the functioning of a wide range of accounting departments. Compare the accounting systems of Tesco with those of a local store, for example.

The list below suggests some areas to investigate, some of the weaknesses that could occur in those areas and some suggested solutions. You should be able to relate this list to the workplace you are using for the Project and add to it.

areas for investigation	possible weaknesses and suggested solutions
sales ledger	late sending out of invoices errors in manually produced invoices poor credit control procedures *possible solution - computerisation*
purchases ledger	late posting of entries to supplier accounts delays in making payments suppliers overcharging fraud caused by employees setting up dummy accounts to which payments are sent *possible solutions - computerisation, tighter checking procedures, using BACS payment systems*
payroll	time taken and errors incurred in manual payroll fraud caused by employees reporting false hours or changing figures *possible solutions - computerisation, tighter checking procedures*
costing	confusion in the use of coding poorly designed job sheets *possible solutions - reorganisation of coding and cost centres, redesign of job sheets*
cash handling	inefficient recording of cash and cheque receipts and reconciling of cash held errors in completion of bank paying-in slips fraud from employees helping themselves to cash *possible solutions – tighter checking procedures*

Jot down some ideas and develop a shortlist of topics for discussion with your workplace mentor and assessor.

making the most of your advisers

It is important to make the most of the advice which can be given. Talk to your **workplace mentor** about your ideas for your Project. Ask if he/she has any other ideas about problem areas in the accounting system where management and procedures could be improved. You may be able to do the organisation a favour by carrying out what will effectively be a free consultancy service!

Talk also to your **assessor**, who is most likely to be your training centre tutor. If you run out of inspiration for ideas, ask for a list of the subjects used for Projects undertaken by other students.

limiting the scope

It is important when choosing a topic for your Project to remember that you are writing 3,000 to 4,000 words – ie six to eight sides of A4 text plus appendices. This is not actually a very long piece of work (although it may feel like it at the time). This means that you should **limit the scope** of what you are writing about to a specific area and not try to cover too much or be too general. Avoid, for example, subjects like the management of the Buying Department of Tesco plc. On the other hand, you should not limit what you are writing about to a very narrow study, for example the cheque signing procedures of a small independent grocery store. It all comes down to common sense and the results of practical discussion with your advisers.

confidentiality

If you are using your own workplace or any other workplace as a basis for your Project you should establish at an early stage with your workplace mentor or manager what information can be used in the Project and what information is confidential and out of bounds.

As mentioned above, you will be expected to include appendices in your Project which will be additional to the 3,000 to 4,000 word target. These appendices might include items such as organisation charts, financial documents, payroll lists, details of customers and suppliers. These will contain sensitive and confidential information. You must obtain clearance from the management of the workplace that you are allowed to reproduce this information in your Project.

You will, however, be able to reassure the workplace management that any Project will be treated as confidential by the assessment centre and any external verifier from AAT.

COVERING THE PERFORMANCE CRITERIA IN THE PROJECT

When writing the Project you will need to be familiar with the **performance criteria** of Elements 10.1 and 10.2. It is useful to produce some form of grid which will set out columns for:

- the performance criteria
- a brief description of the evidence produced

The AAT Student Record for NVQ route students, which is available for download at www.aat.co.uk (Student Resources), is often used for this purpose. An extract from the Student Record is shown below.

	Performance criteria - in order to perform this element successfully you need to			
A	Plan work activities to make the optimum use of resources and to ensure that work is completed within agreed timescales			
B	Review the competence of individuals undertaking work activities and arrange the necessary training			
C	Prepare, in collaboration with management, **contingency plans** to meet possible emergencies			
D	Communicate work methods and schedules to colleagues in ways that help them to understand what is expected of them			
E	Monitor work activities sufficiently closely to ensure that quality standards are being met			

In the section that follows we will take each performance criterion in turn and suggest ways in which you can produce the evidence in the Project. Please note two points:

- we will also list the 'Range' items which require to be evidenced ('Range' items form part of the specifications and explain words and phrases printed in bold type in the performance criteria)
- we will start with Element 10.2 and finish with 10.1, which seems the more logical order from the point of view of content

Element 10.2

Identify opportunities for improving the effectiveness of an accounting system

'The second element is about identifying weaknesses in an accounting system and making recommendations to rectify these. This involves identifying potential for misuse of a system, whether this is accidental (errors) or deliberate (fraud). You are also required to update the system, for example to comply with legislative requirements, and to check that the output is correct after the system has been updated.'

performance criteria

In order to perform this element successfully you need to:

A Identify **weaknesses** and potential for improvements to the **accounting system** and consider their impact on the operation of the organisation.

Comment:

This performance criterion relates directly to the subject of your Project. The evidence will be found in the initial analysis you make of the organisation. This could take the form of a SWOT analysis (see page 39). The weaknesses will be found in areas where management of the system could be improved. The symptoms of these weaknesses will be found in two types of system specified in the Range:

- systems which open up **potential for errors**, eg areas in which supervision may be insufficient or areas where new procedures should be introduced to prevent errors occurring

- systems where there is **exposure to possible fraud**, again these will be in areas where supervision may be insufficient or where new procedures should be introduced to prevent fraud occurring

The two types of accounting system to be analysed are also mentioned in the Range:

- a **manual** accounting system

- a **computerised** system

B Identify potential areas of fraud arising from control avoidance within the accounting system and grade the risk

Comment:

This performance criterion should also be covered by the initial analysis of the organisation. It develops an area covered by the previous performance criterion, ie the potential for **fraud** in the accounting system. This could occur when management control is not as tight as it could be (eg checking procedures are not adhered to) or where those checking procedures are not in place. An example of this could be where cash received is checked by the same person each day. A more secure system is one where the cash is checked by a second person.

Note that there is a requirement to grade the fraud risk, preferably using a matrix. This is explained on pages 80 - 81 which deal with fraud as part of the required Knowledge & Understanding for the Unit (items 2,3,7).

C   Review methods of operating regularly in respect of their cost-effectiveness, reliability and speed

Comment:

Your final recommendations in the Project for improving an aspect of the accounting system should incorporate a timetable for monitoring the success of the suggested measures, eg a monthly, three monthly or six monthly review by management. The key aspects that need to be considered are:

- **cost-effectiveness** – your recommendations for change should include assessment of cost-effectiveness (ie 'value for money') and part of the review process should include a regular analysis of costs and related performance indicators – this is explained further on pages 66 and 67 (Knowledge & Understanding item 6).
- **reliability** and **speed** – these are measures of how well the new system is working, for example the number of errors made against the target (reliability), the number of invoices processed in a day against the target (speed)

It is appreciated that in many cases you will not be able to monitor success in this way because you will not be in the workplace. It is sufficient that you set down guidelines for these checks by management in your Project recommendations, ie the nature and frequency of the checks.

It should be mentioned here that when deciding how to improve the accounting system you should carry out a **cost benefit analysis** of the proposed change. This is a planning aid which assesses the costs of any change. These costs include items such as new equipment, software, premises costs and staff training. The costs will be assessed to answer the question 'will the benefits resulting from the change justify the costs?' For the purposes of evidence you will not always be able to quote figures, but it is important to show that you have taken costs into consideration when coming to a decision about the change. You could, for example, list the costs by description to show that you have considered them.

Note that **cost benefit analysis** is not quite the same as **cost-effectiveness** which involves a regular monitoring of costs and related performance indicators to ensure that the organisation is getting 'value for money' on an ongoing basis (see above).

D   Make **recommendations** to the appropriate person in a clear, easily understood format

Comment:

This relates to your final recommendations in the Project for improving an aspect of the accounting system. The Range requires that there should be evidence which is **oral** (word of mouth) and **written**. Oral evidence could be a signed statement from the workplace management that recommendations have been made; written recommendations are likely to embodied in the text of the Project itself in the form of the Executive Summary (see also PC 10.2E and page 37). The important words in the performance criterion are 'clear' and 'easily understood'. This is an exercise in management communication.

Again, it is appreciated that your recommendations may be purely hypothetical, ie 'if I were a manager in this situation, I would recommend the following . . .'

Oral communication could be evidenced by something along the lines of 'I would speak to the employees and tell them the following . . ' and the written format is likely to be the report format you are adopting.

E Ensure recommendations are supported by a clear rationale which includes an explanation of any assumption made

Comment:

Your Project should include a clear rationale (an argued explanation) of your recommendations for change and improvements in the accounting system. In simple terms: 'this is what I recommend and these are my reasons, based on my analysis of the present accounting system.' This rationale could be evidenced in an 'Executive Summary' which will supplement the Project (see page 37). This is a succinct summary (no more than a page) of the report and its conclusions, stressing:

*   the nature of the problem(s), the possible and preferred solutions
*   the outcomes, ie your recommendations for change and the ways in which they have affected the organisation

F Update the system in accordance with **changes** that affect the way the system should operate and check that your update is producing the required results

Comment:

This performance criterion requires you to show that the changes to the accounting system that you recommend can result from two pressures for change specified in the Range:

*   **external regulations**

*   **organisational policies and procedures**

Pressures for change could be **external** – for example the requirements of the Data Protection Act relating to the processing of personal data, VAT regulations, and the operation of online retailing. **Internal** pressures for change could include changes in organisational structure (eg re-organisation of the Accounts Department) and procedures (eg the introduction of online ordering or changes in the supply chain). Your evidence must therefore show an awareness of the pressures affecting your chosen workplace.

The second part of the performance criterion requires you to check that the results of your proposals are periodically checked to ensure that your changes are producing the required results. This ties in with performance criterion C (see previous page) which requires evidence of a system of a regular review of methods of operation.

Again, it is appreciated that your changes may not actually take place in the real world and so evidence for this performance criterion could be along the line of 'if the changes were introduced, then the internal and external pressures would be . . .' and 'the following checks would be made to ensure that the changes are producing the required results . . .'

Note: if you are studying this Unit through the NVQ assessment route, Performance Criterion F has now been amended to:

'Explain to those affected the implications of **recommended changes** in terms of financial costs and benefits.'

This change demands a more financial slant to the requirement (see the text on the previous page relating to **cost benefit analysis** in Performance Criterion C).

Element 10.1

Co-ordinate work activities within the accounting environment

'The first element requires you to co-ordinate work activities effectively within the accounting environment. This includes setting realistic objectives, targets and deadlines and managing people in such a way that these can be met. You also need to show that you prepare contingency plans to cover a variety of problems that can reduce the likelihood of meeting objectives, targets and deadlines.'

performance criteria

In order to perform this element successfully you need to:

A Plan work activities to make the optimum use of resources and to ensure that work is completed within agreed timescales

Comment:

The evidence for this performance criterion should ideally be based on the **work routines in the workplace** required by your planned changes to an accounting system. The need for managers to develop planning and time management skills is set out in the Knowledge & Understanding requirements:

- methods of work planning and scheduling (item 4)
- personal time management techniques (item 5)

These are covered in detail on pages 61-66.

Optimising 'resources' here relates to the best use you will make of:

- people (human resources)
- premises and equipment (capital resources)
- materials
- information

These relate to Knowledge & Understanding item 14 'The control of resources by individuals within the organisation' (see pages 58-59) and will be measured by 'cost-effective' performance indicators (see pages 66-67).

Another source of evidence for this performance criterion approved by AAT is **the use of the Project itself**, ie the planning and scheduling processes that you will undertake to complete the Project on schedule and to the required standard. If you adopt this approach you will need to ensure that your planning processes – including the use of resources – are well documented.

You will need to draw up an action plan with key dates and targets and record progress. You will also need to list resources such as:

- your training centre assessor and workplace mentor
- course training materials
- your time (including any learning centre computer time)

You will need to show in your evidence that you have made the best use of these resources and have completed the Project on time. These targets that you set will be a way of measuring your personal cost-effectiveness.

B Review the competence of individuals undertaking work activities and arrange the necessary training

Comment:

This is another performance criterion with a reality gap. If you are in a management position in an accounting environment you should as a matter of course review employee competence on a regular basis, interview employees and discuss and arrange training. If you are instrumental in bringing about a change to the accounting system, retraining will become an essential process. This is all part of management responsibility.

If, however, you are currently training as an accounting technician, it is unlikely you will have the luxury of being in this position. In this case you will have to state in your Project recommendations for a change in an accounting system that you will need to review employee competence, interview employees and discuss and arrange training. For example, if you are computerising a sales ledger function, you will need to arrange external training in the use of the computer hardware and software. If you are changing internal procedures you are more likely to have to arrange internal training for employees.

Note that external training will have a cost implication to be taken into account in any cost benefit analysis you carry out (see page 21). You could include quotations for external training courses as evidence in your Appendix.

C Prepare, in collaboration with management, **contingency plans** to meet possible emergencies

Comment:

An important aspect of management skills is the ability to deal with situations when well laid plans cannot function properly when the expected situation changes. When this happens a competent manager should be able to set **contingency** (alternative) plans into action. A good manager should already have thought these through. The Range in the specifications define three situations where contingency planning will be needed:

- **a fully functioning computer system not being available**
- **staff absence**
- **changes in work patterns and demands**

You should provide evidence of what you would do in all three cases, for example:

- complete and permanent computer failure may result in the need to go back to a manual system, temporary failure may require rescheduling of work and possible overtime working
- staff absence is a common problem and is normally solved by redistribution of duties amongst other employees
- changes in work patterns and demands may require the redeployment of staff or even redundancies; busy times may require the employment of temporary staff

This area is covered on pages 61-62, which deal with Knowledge & Understanding item 4 'Methods of work planning and scheduling'.

As far as this performance criterion is concerned you will have to state in your Project recommendations that you will need to plan for these three contingencies when you change the accounting system. For example you may need to retain a manual system when computerisation takes place, in case the new technology fails. You may need to arrange for staff to be trained and multi-skilled to cover for absence. You may need to plan ahead to recruit temps at busy times. These are subjects which could usefully be discussed with a workplace manager or mentor.

D Communicate work methods and schedules to colleagues in ways that help them to understand what is expected of them

Comment:

Another important aspect of management skills is the ability to communicate to your colleagues details of changes in working methods and to impress upon them the need to keep to schedules.

This relates closely to Knowledge & Understanding requirements:

- item 9 'Principles of supervision and delegation'
- item 10 'Principles of creating effective inter-personal relationships, team building and staff motivation'

These items are discussed on pages 70-73.

Evidence for this performance criterion could be a statement in your recommendations that your plans should ensure that this takes place, possibly by calling a meeting of employees, briefing them about the changes, providing them with schedules and encouraging discussion and questioning.

E Monitor work activities sufficiently closely to ensure that quality standards are being met

Comment:

Managers are responsible for the maintenance of quality standards in an organisation. In an accounting environment 'quality' can relate to a number of areas, eg customer service when employees answer the telephone, the number of sales orders processed in a time period, the acceptable number of errors in a stated number of sales invoices, and so on.

Evidence for this performance criterion could take the form of a statement in the recommendations for the changed accounting system that quality standards will be set and monitored. It would be useful to give some examples of individual standards.

F Co-ordinate work activities effectively and in accordance with work plans and contingency plans

Comment:

This requires a simple statement that the management has organised and implemented the changes in accordance with the schedule. It should note any contingency plans that have been put into action and explain the reasons for any change in plan.

G Encourage colleagues to report to you promptly any problems and queries that are beyond their authority or expertise to resolve, and resolve these where they are within your authority and expertise

H Refer problems and queries to the appropriate person where resolution is beyond your authority or expertise

Comment:

These two performance criteria are included together because they refer to the same aspect of management skills – encouraging communication with colleagues and superiors.

They are also linked to Knowledge & Understanding item 10 'Principles of creating effective inter-personal relationships, team building and staff motivation' (see pages 70-73).

Evidence for the performance criteria could relate to actual situations that have occurred in the workplace (in which case they should be documented) or the points could be incorporated in the employee meeting suggested for the evidence for performance criterion D 'Communicate work methods and schedules to colleagues in ways that help them to understand what is expected of them'. If the points are incorporated into the meeting they should be communicated to colleagues as a definite policy, eg 'Let me know if you have a problem. I will either deal with it myself, or if I can't, I will pass it on to someone who can. The important point is that you let me know straightaway if you have a problem. There is no point sitting on it.

THE WOOD AND THE TREES

The last few pages (pages 20 to 26) contain important pointers to what you should be putting in your report to cover the performance criteria of Unit 10. It is important that you bear all these in mind, because all this evidence will need to go into your Project.

But you may be feeling that having read all this, you cannot 'see the wood for the trees' and are unable to envisage what exactly has to go in the Project, and where it should go. In other words, you have too much detail in your mind and no real idea of the shape of the whole thing. The diagram on the next page attempts to set out in visual form in basic terms 'what you have to do and where it has to go.'

It assumes the ideal situation for assessment purposes – you have based your Project on a real workplace and have been able to implement an improvement in the accounting system and have then been able, as a manager, to assess its success. If you do not have access to a workplace, as mentioned elsewhere in this chapter, or if you are not a manager, you will need to adopt an element of 'make believe' and assume that you are.

We will also link the Knowledge & Understanding evidence to this structure later in this text – please see page 49.

Now study the 'wood and the trees' diagram on the next page.

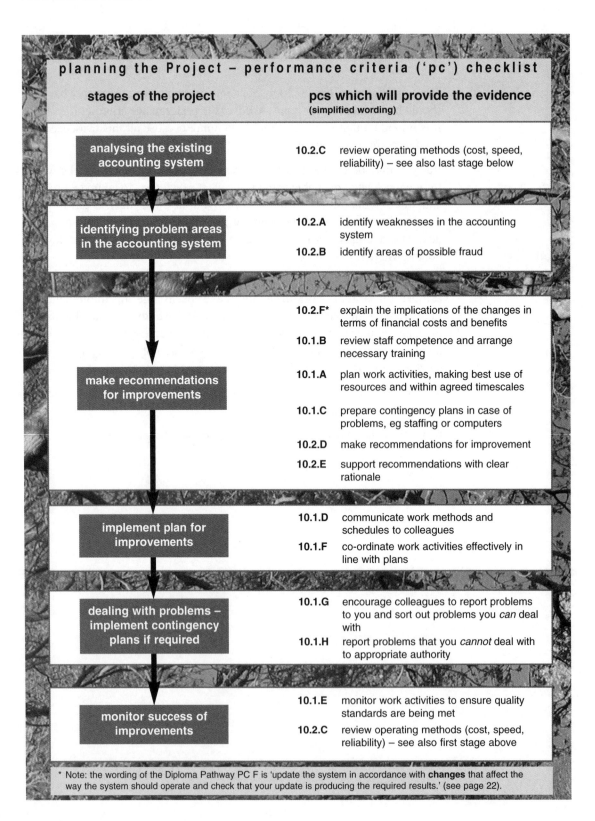

planning the Project – performance criteria ('pc') checklist

stages of the project	pcs which will provide the evidence (simplified wording)

| **analysing the existing accounting system** | **10.2.C** review operating methods (cost, speed, reliability) – see also last stage below |

| **identifying problem areas in the accounting system** | **10.2.A** identify weaknesses in the accounting system
 10.2.B identify areas of possible fraud |

| **make recommendations for improvements** | **10.2.F*** explain the implications of the changes in terms of financial costs and benefits
 10.1.B review staff competence and arrange necessary training
 10.1.A plan work activities, making best use of resources and within agreed timescales
 10.1.C prepare contingency plans in case of problems, eg staffing or computers
 10.2.D make recommendations for improvement
 10.2.E support recommendations with clear rationale |

| **implement plan for improvements** | **10.1.D** communicate work methods and schedules to colleagues
 10.1.F co-ordinate work activities effectively in line with plans |

| **dealing with problems – implement contingency plans if required** | **10.1.G** encourage colleagues to report problems to you and sort out problems you *can* deal with
 10.1.H report problems that you *cannot* deal with to appropriate authority |

| **monitor success of improvements** | **10.1.E** monitor work activities to ensure quality standards are being met
 10.2.C review operating methods (cost, speed, reliability) – see also first stage above |

* Note: the wording of the Diploma Pathway PC F is 'update the system in accordance with **changes** that affect the way the system should operate and check that your update is producing the required results.' (see page 22).

Student Guidance

guidance notes

1 Ensure that you now have a shortlist of topics which you could use as a subject for your Project and which will enable you to identify a 'favourite' topic.

Discuss these potential topics with

(a)   your workplace mentor

(b)   your training provider assessor

(c)   your fellow students, if this is possible

Following on from this process you should choose your topic.

2 Ensure that you are familiar with the performance criteria. Read through the text in this chapter (pages 19 to 26) and use the diagram on the previous page to help you. Make rough notes relating to the stages shown on the diagram, suggesting the evidence that you will need to produce for each stage. You might find it useful to use a separate page for each stage.

Note that the evidence for the Knowledge & Understanding content, mentioned in the text of this chapter (pages 19 to 26), will be covered in Chapters 4, 5 and 6 of this book. At this stage, however, you should concentrate on what the performance criteria require.

3 You will need at this stage to deal with the confidentiality issue. Before proceeding any further you will need to obtain permission from the appropriate workplace to reproduce the information you need for your report. You will need to speak to your workplace mentor, or, if you are basing your report on someone else's workplace, the appropriate manager or adviser.

If you are using an AAT Simulation, which should be adopted only as a last resort, you will obviously not need to worry about confidentiality. All the other recommendations, however, still apply.

The next chapter deals with the practicalities of the format and writing of the report, including the need to draw up a schedule and targets for completion of the various parts of the Project.

As mentioned above, you will also need to study Chapters 4, 5 and 6, which cover the Knowledge & Understanding content which also forms part of the evidence.

3 Writing the project

This chapter offers practical advice on the assessment of the Unit and the writing of the Project. It covers:

- the context of the Project in the assessment process

- the structure of the Project – the sections that it contains

- the writing process – keeping to 4,000 words

- the writing style to be used

- the contents of the various sections of the Project

- establishing a plan and a time schedule for the Project

- the individual responsibilities of the student, assessor and workplace mentor

In the next Section of this book 'The Theory behind the Project' (pages 47-84) we will explain the Knowledge & Understanding evidence that needs to be incorporated if possible into the Project.

PERFORMANCE CRITERIA COVERED

unit 10:
MANAGING SYSTEMS AND PEOPLE IN THE ACCOUNTING ENVIRONMENT

Element 10.1   **Manage people within the accounting environment**

Element 10.2   **Identify opportunities for improving the effectiveness of an accounting system**

This chapter is a practical guide to project writing and therefore does not cover any of the performance criteria or Knowledge & Understanding requirements of Unit 10

THE PROJECT AND THE ASSESSMENT PROCESS

It is important to remember that the Project forms just part of the overall Unit 10 assessment. The complete assessment requirements are:

- the writing of the **Project**, which should normally contain 3,000 to 4,000 words

- a signed declaration from your employer – an '**employer testimony**' ('letter of authenticity') which confirms that the Project is your own original work and aims to improve the quality and management of the accounting system; if you are not in employment, the testimony should be signed by the manager of the workplace you have investigated

- answers to **assessor questioning** to verify the contents of the Project and to assess any areas of Knowledge & Understanding or other evidence not covered in the project or in its appendices

The Project is therefore at the core of the assessment and you will make life much easier for yourself if you provide as much evidence as you can in the report.

Most Centres will provide some form of checklist so that you can tick off the required evidence as it is generated in the writing of the Project. As noted in the last chapter, the AAT Student Record will chart the coverage of performance criteria and range.

A similar record sheet or 'tick list' can carry out the same function for the required Knowledge & Understanding.

STRUCTURE OF THE PROJECT – AN OVERVIEW

The Project should normally be presented in standard **report format**. A summary of a recommended format is shown on the next page. It is adapted and expanded from a template produced by the AAT.

Report headings, such as the ones shown on the summary, may vary according to the format adopted and from organisation to organisation, but the critical point is that all the elements of a standard report should be present. It should be a closely argued document; if anything is left out, it will fail to communicate its findings and conclusions effectively.

We will cover the required writing style in detail on pages 33 to 34. All you need to appreciate at this point is that a report is a formal document and not a personal reflection. It should be formal in structure, in page layout and in its language.

SUGGESTED REPORT FORMAT

title page   a statement of what the Project is about, quoting your student name and membership number

list of contents   a full list of all the Project sections with page references

terms of reference   why the report is being written – to cover Unit 10 and also to improve an accounting system

executive summary   a short summary of the report (stressing its conclusions) designed to be read by the management of the organisation concerned

methodology   how you planned and went about compiling the information for the report, acknowledging and thanking the people who helped you

organisation background a factual summary of what the organisation does, its products, customers, suppliers and stakeholders

analysis of current system an analysis of the strengths and weaknesses of the accounting system and how they affect the organisation, plus an identification of areas where errors and fraud could occur

findings   results of research you have carried out (eg questionnaires) and relation to any management theories that are relevant

recommendations   possible solutions to the area(s) of weakness, involving a cost benefit analysis, choice of preferred course of action and an implementation plan

implementation & review an evaluation of the success of the implementation of the recommendations to improve the accounting system (where they have been made)

appendices   extra material such as organisation charts, questionnaires and documents

The individual sections of the report format shown above are described in detail on pages 35-40.

HINTS ON THE WRITING PROCESS

what is 4000 words?

The upper limit of your report is 4,000 words. You will be relieved to hear that this does not require a very long report. A normal page might contain 500 words on average, so 4,000 words will fill eight pages of normal word-processed text. You should aim for a length of 3,000 to 4,000, ie between six and eight pages. The 4,000 word limit does not include the appendices, so you are free to include as much supporting material as you need, but it must be relevant and you must take care to avoid any breaches of confidentiality if you include copies of internal documents and accounting data.

word-processed format

It is important that the report is word-processed. It will look more professional, and it will make it much easier to manage and to amend as you start writing. A word-processing program such as Word will also enable you to carry out regular spellchecks and word counts.

Also note that:

- the sections (eg 'Terms of Reference', 'Methodology') should each start on a new page
- the sections and the paragraphs *could* be numbered; eg if 'Methodology' is Section 4, the paragraphs in that Section will be numbered 4.1, 4.2, 4.3, and so on.

writing style

A formal report requires straightforward written English. There is nothing particularly difficult about producing written English; the problems lie with the current tendency to write as you speak, or as you text, or as you email. The result is often an abbreviated form of written English which as you will appreci8 does nt work 2 well on the page.

Another problem facing people who are not used to writing formal written English is that they think of it as some sort of overblown 'posh' sounding language which has to be complicated and impressive to make its point. Nothing could be further from the truth. The test of good written English is that it should be:

- plain and simple
- to the point
- understandable by a twelve year-old

You might think that the last point is some form of a joke, but you might be surprised to learn that quality newspapers aim for this level of reading ability. To sum up, the first rule of writing is 'keep it simple'. Good writing must be clear. It must get the message across.

hints on writing plain English in a report

- use **simple words** instead of complicated ones
- use **short sentences** instead of long ones
- use the **active tense** rather than the passive, eg 'the line manager *carries out* regular checks on the petty cash book' rather than 'regular checks *are carried out* on the petty cash book by the line manager'
- use the **third person** (he, she, it) rather than 'I' or 'we' – remember that the report should be a formal analysis rather than 'this is what I think about . . .'
- **avoid slang** eg 'the line manager really *hacked off* the rest of the staff'; you should use the word 'annoyed' instead of 'hacked' to avoid the innocent reader assuming that some form of workplace massacre had taken place
- avoid **abbreviations** such as 'isn't', didn't' and write the phrases in full: 'is not' and 'did not'
- avoid **jargon** and **acronyms** which may not be understood by the general reader, for example 'the FD disapproved of the BOGOF policy because it reduced margins' which means 'the Finance Director disapproved of the 'buy one, get one free' policy because it reduced margins'

other practical report writing hints

You may find that you will end up cutting material to keep within the limit. Remember that the important material is your analysis of the accounting system, your recommendations for change and any analysis of the changes made. If you need to make cuts, they should be from the introductory sections which describe the organisation, its products, customers, suppliers and stakeholders.

Remember to back-up your work each time you work on your report. There are too many sad stories such as 'I did my report on my lap-top, but the hard disk corrupted and I lost the lot.'

Read what you have written. Print out copies of what you have done as you go along so that you can check your work.

Ask other people to read what you have written to make sure that the reader can understand your meaning. Your workplace mentor and assessor will obviously read what you write, but it is useful to ask a friend or a partner as well, as long as you do not endanger a lifelong relationship in the process.

SECTIONS OF THE REPORT

On the next few pages we will illustrate the various sections of the Project report, all of which should start on a new page. We will explain what the headings mean and give an idea of what should be included in each section.

Remember that report headings and formats are likely to vary from one organisation to another. The format shown here is often used, although the same basic structure should be common to any report. You should adopt the format you are used to, or, if you are not familiar with any format, you would be advised to adopt the format illustrated here (based on an AAT model).

title page

The title page should state:

- what the Project is about
- the purpose of the Project
- your name
- your AAT student membership number
- the date of submission

The title should *not* be 'AAT Unit 10'.

An example is shown below.

An analysis of the manual accounting operations of Didgeree Limited with recommendations for conversion to a Sage Line 50 computer accounting system.

Submitted by: A S Tudent

AAT student membership number: N001999

Date: March 2007

This report is submitted for assessment of Unit 10 'Managing Systems and People in the Accounting Environment'.

list of contents

The list of contents should list each section, including the appendices, in page order and give accurate page references.

Note that every section should start on a new page. This will mean, of course, that the Project will run to more than the eight pages that 4,000 words will normally fill as solid text.

List of Contents

	page
Terms of reference	1
Executive summary	2
Methodology	3
Background to Didgeree Limited	4
The accounting function of Didgeree Limited	6

. . . and so on

---

terms of reference

The terms of reference outline the **reasons for writing the report**. These are:

- why the Project is required – ie it is part of your assessment of Unit 10
- the objectives of the Project set out by AAT – ie what you are hoping to achieve in the Project

Note the use of paragraph numbering and bullet points to clarify the text.

Terms of Reference

1 This Project has been prepared to cover the assessment requirements of AAT Unit 10 'Managing systems and people in the accounting environment'.

2 The objectives of this Project are to:

- analyse the manual accounting system of Didgeree Limited in order to identify areas of weakness
- make recommendations for improving the accounting system through the introduction of a computerised system
- assess the success of the recommended changes

executive summary

This is likely to be one of the last sections that you write. It is a report summary written for the senior (executive) management of the organisation involved. The object of the summary is to set out in a nutshell:

- the analysis that took place – eg of a manual accounting system
- the changes recommended (and made) to the accounting system – eg through the computerisation of various sections of the accounting system, using Sage Line 50
- a conclusion analysing the effect of the changes on the organisation – the benefits (speed, accuracy, better and up-to-date management information) outweighing the costs (hardware, software, training)

This summary need be no more than a page of text, presented in succinct paragraphs. Remember that the management reading the summary will be very familiar with the organisation (they manage it, after all) and will also be short of time!

methodology

This section is also sometimes headed 'Procedures'. It briefly describes the research methods used in producing the report. This section should include:

- a brief description of the way in which you analysed the accounting system and consulted with the people managing it and working within it, eg by observation, monitoring, questionnaire, interview
- details of any people from outside the organisation that you used as an information source, eg customers, computer consultants
- use of any 'written' sources, eg books, manuals, websites (note that you should not list them here, but include details on the appendices)

It is normal and polite practice to acknowledge and thank in this section all the people you have consulted.

organisation background

This section is often the first part of the Project that you will write as it is easy to put together and will get rid of the blank sheet of paper syndrome.

What is required here is a *brief* description of the organisation which is the subject of your report. Details you could include are:

- its name and location
- legal status (eg limited company, local authority department, charity)
- how long it has been functioning
- what it does: its main 'products' and 'markets'

- its customers
- main competitors
- its stakeholders (ie others who may have an interest of some kind in the organisation), eg the public, regulatory authorities, pressure groups
- structure of the organisation – where the accounting function fits in (you could include an organisation chart in the appendices)

Remember that this section is intended to 'set the scene' and should not be overburdened with too much detail. Remember also that the Project is a report to management, and they will presumably know about most of what you include in this section. Clear bullet point presentation will help in this section, for example . . .

Organisation background

- Didgeree Limited is a limited company, established in 1985 in Milburn, West Midlands.

- Its main business is the importation and marketing of Australian giftware through its 'Boomerang' wholesale and mail order operations. Its customers are UK retail stores and mail order buyers. It has no significant UK competitor.

- Its main stakeholders are the import regulatory authorities and environmental pressure groups who have objected to the sale of goods made from possum skins.

- Didgeree Limited is organised into departments (including Accounting Department) – see Appendix 5 on page 22 for a structure chart.

---

analysis of the current system

This section should start with a brief description of the workings of the Accounting Department. Again, a structure chart can be included in the Appendices. The details might include:

- the different sections of the Department, eg Purchases Ledger, Sales Ledger, Payroll and the approximate number of people employed
- where you fit into the Department (if you work in it)

But the important part of this section is your **analysis** of the Accounting Department and the highlighting of weaknesses.

A useful starting point for this analysis is the SWOT approach. 'SWOT' is a traditional management analytical technique. The letters stand for the identification of **s**trengths, **w**eaknesses, **o**pportunities and **t**hreats.

Strengths	These are the 'plus' points of the accounting system and its management – for example an integrated computer accounting system which saves time and money, an efficient checking procedure or well trained staff.
Weaknesses	These are the areas that you will need to identify in order to carry out improvements to the accounting system. These weaknesses could be identified in a manual accounting system and also in a computerised accounting system. They might include, for example, lack of training and insufficient staffing or previous generation computer hardware which is incompatible with new software. They might open up the possibility of errors and fraud.
Opportunities	These are areas of an organisation (the accounting system in this case) which could be improved and developed and become the 'strengths', the 'plus' points. For example a manual accounting system could be computerised.
Threats	Threats are external to the accounting system and could include possible outsourcing of accounting activities or a merger with another organisation.

findings

These follow on from your analysis of the present accounting system and identification of weaknesses. They could include the results of any employee questionnaire(s) and the application of relevant theories (eg motivation).

recommendations

This section will set out what you think are the causes of the problem(s), suggest possible solutions and choose a preferred option with the help of a cost benefit analysis (see page 21). This need not involve actual figures (although this can be attempted), but should weigh up the costs (eg new computers and training) and show the benefits (long-term efficiencies).

This section should include a detailed action plan for the implementation of the changes.

implementation and review

This section assumes that you are able to implement the suggested changes. It should incorporate:

- a timetable for monitoring the success of the changes
- a method of monitoring the changes in respect of reliability and speed (eg number of errors per hundred invoices processed and number of invoices processed per day)
- an assessment of the success of the implemented changes

As mentioned before in this text, it is very possible that you will not in reality be able to implement the changes you have suggested. If this is the case, you should ask your assessor to arrange an alternative form of assessment.

This might take the form of a 'what-if' scenario based on your Project and require you to write down what you would do in those circumstances. In other words, you pretend that the changes have taken place and you indicate your responses to possible but imaginary outcomes.

Alternatively you may be asked questions in an interview situation about what you would expect to happen in various circumstances and your response will be recorded as evidence.

appendices

Appendices:

- are not included in the final word count
- should be numbered
- should be cross-referenced where appropriate in the text
- should be relevant to the subject matter of the Project
- may include confidential material and so it is essential that the permission of the relevant organisation is given before material can be used

Examples of appendices include:

- structure charts of the organisation and its accounting system
- relevant financial documents, eg sample invoices
- budgets
- internal memoranda
- minutes of meetings
- questionnaires used and analyses of findings from the questionnaires

As noted above, the appendices should be relevant and refer to the text of the Project. Avoid the temptation to use the appendices as a dumping ground for excess material.

and do not forget . . . your letter of authenticity

If the Project is based on a real workplace you will need a letter from your workplace manager – an employer testimony – to authenticate your Project; it should state that:

- the Project is all your own work
- the confidentiality aspects have been covered

The letter must be:

- on headed paper and dated
- signed by the workplace manager, with his/her name and job title

An example letter of authenticity is shown below.

Didgeree Limited
Unit 3 Bush Industrial Estate
Ramsay Road
Milburn
WM6 5FG

Tel 01901 456271 Fax 01901 457829

J H Potter
Department of Professional Studies
Milburn College of Technology
Forest Road
Milburn
WM3 6RA

1 April 2005

Dear Mr Potter

Accounting Systems Project

This is to testify that Jos Cobber is a Finance Assistant in the Accounting Department at Didgeree Limited.

Jos Cobber has undertaken this project, during the performance of her work, with the aim of improving the quality and management of the accounting system of the company.

This confirms that the project is Jos Cobber's original work and that she has the permission of Didgeree Limited to reproduce the data contained in the body of the report and in the appendices.

Yours sincerely

J Kennedy

J Kennedy, Accounts Manager

TIME PLANNING

In the first chapter of this book we illustrated the processes needed for the successful completion of your Project, using the diagram reproduced on the next page. It is worth studying this diagram again so that you can get an overview of **what** is required and **when**.

Efficient **time planning** is essential so that you can get going as soon as possible. You will ideally need to finish the Project by the end of April in order that it can be assessed and approved in time to allow you to revise for your June examinations.

The timetable shown below is only a suggestion, based on College practice. You should check to see if it ties in with your teaching Centre's requirements. It assumes that you start your course in September/October. You may find, for example, that your Centre allows 18 months for completion, in which case this suggested schedule will need amending.

October
Decide on your subject – in discussion with your assessor and workplace mentor.

November
Make a start – write **the first 500 words** – this would ideally be the description of the organisation you have chosen for the Project. Let your assessor comment on what you have written.

December
If the Project is proceeding well, **keep working on it** and try to complete as much as you can before the New Year.

If your recommendations can be carried out they should be completed as soon as possible so that their effectiveness can be assessed.

March
You should ideally have **finished the first draft** of the complete Project by the beginning of March so that it can be handed in to your assessor.

You should then have a **preliminary assessor interview** by the end of March. At this stage you should identify any Performance Criteria, Range or Knowledge & Understanding items which are missing from the evidence so that you can make plans to produce the appropriate evidence.

April
The Project should now be 'tweaked' to provide the missing evidence and a **final assessor interview** held, during which evidence can be produced, if required, through supplementary questioning.

suggested Unit 10 assessment plan

choosing workplace
or other organisation
to assess
as the basis of the report

choosing subject area
within the accounting system
- evaluating system and use of people
- improving system and use of people
- assessing success of changes

using experience
- own management
experience, or
- observing managers, or,
- AAT Simulation (fall back)

**suggested
schedule**

October

**AGREE SUBJECT
WITH ASSESSOR**

consulting with people
- workplace mentor
or manager
- college assessor
- timescale
- content
- resources needed

November

**THE FIRST 500
WORDS**

learning from this book
- about the format and
style of the report
- about what you need to
include in the report
- about the background
Knowledge and
Understanding

Feb/March

**DRAFT PROJECT
COMPLETED**

end-March

**preliminary assessor
interview**

checking
report covers pcs,
range and Knowledge
and Understanding

April

**FINAL PROJECT
COMPLETION**

**producing extra
evidence**
to cover pcs, range,
Knowledge and
Understanding not in the
report, eg with oral or
written questioning

**final assessor
interview**

RESPONSIBILITIES FOR THE PROJECT

Although it is the student who has to write the Project, it is important to appreciate that the responsibilities for its successful completion are shared with the assessor and the workplace mentor/manager. The responsibilities for the Project are summarised below.

student responsibilities

Some teaching centres recommend that the student draws up a formal assessment plan setting out the various tasks and deadlines as agreed with the assessor. This plan is then signed by the student. A possible format is . . .

ASSESSMENT PLAN

Task	Planned completion date	Actual completion date

I confirm I have agreed to the planned completion dates and will do my best to meet them.

signed   ....

name   ....

date   ....

Tasks that could be listed in this plan include:

- choose the subject for the Project
- choose a workplace mentor
- write the first 500 words
- complete research
- complete first draft
- map content against Performance Criteria, Range and Knowledge & Understanding

- preliminary assessor interview
- produce any extra evidence required
- final assessor interview

Further responsibilities of the student include:

- meeting with the assessor at agreed times
- liaising with the workplace mentor/manager when necessary
- ensuring that any confidentiality issues have been sorted out

assessor responsibilities

The assessor's overall responsibility is to guide the student through the assessment process to a successful completion of the Project and the required evidence. Specific responsibilities to each student include:

- planning a realistic assessment programme
- agreeing the subject of the Project through one-to-one sessions with the student
- monitoring the production of evidence and ensuring that it is the student's own work
- checking the evidence against the requirements
- carrying out a preliminary assessment interview based on the Project first draft
- providing any additional assessment opportunities that may be necessary
- assessing the Project final version
- carrying out the final assessment interview

workplace mentor responsibilities

The workplace mentor – who may be your boss or a senior employee in the area you are investigating – fulfils an important role in helping you complete your Project. This person should:

- help you initially identify the workplace problems which you will try to remedy through the recommendations in your Project
- help you to obtain the evidence you need
- if possible, read through what you have written
- resolve any problems of confidentiality of information
- authenticate your work (see page 41 for a sample authentication letter)

Student Guidance

guidance notes

1   Ensure that you have identified a suitable report format for your project. This can be a format used by your own organisation, or you can adopt the format shown in this chapter (see page 32).

2   Make sure that you know in your own mind what the maximum of 4,000 words represents.

3   Ensure that you have access to a suitable word-processing package, that you can print out drafts of your work, and, very importantly, that you can back-up your work.

4   Construct a time plan or an assessment plan. Make sure that your deadlines are firmly in your mind.

5   Remember to start each new section on a new page.

6   Read through your own work regularly and ask yourself 'Is this written in simple English? Can it be easily understood?'

7   Ask other people to read through your own work and ask them the same questions: 'Is this written in simple English? Can it be easily understood?'

8   As you write your report ensure that you are referencing it, as you go along, to the Performance Criteria, Range and Knowledge & Understanding items.

9   Organise your appendices efficiently. Make references to them in the text where appropriate. Only include relevant material.

10   Arrange to party when you have completed your Project.

Section 3

The theory behind the Project

This Section contains three chapters:

Chapter 4   The organisation

Chapter 5   Management techniques and theory

Chapter 6   External regulation and dealing with fraud

This Section provides the Knowledge and Understanding background to Unit 10. It follows a logical progression, starting with an overview of the organisation and then focusing in on the issues dealt with in the accounting environment, including:

■ the way in which the accounting function 'fits into' the overall structure of an organisation

■ the way in which the organisation should ideally be managed

■ methods of assessing the risk of fraud and minimising its occurrence

A list of the Knowledge and Understanding items indexed to the pages on which they appear follows on page 48. A guide diagram to where they 'fit' into the various stages of the Project is shown on page 49.

Questions on all three chapters, related to the individual Knowledge and Understanding item requirements are set out on pages 85 to 100.

Knowledge and Understanding: text references

The full Knowledge and Understanding (K&U) requirements of Unit 10 are set out below. The page references are to the coverage of these items in the text.

Students taking the NVQ assessment route should note that a new K&U requirement 9 has been added: 'Techniques for reviewing recommendations through cost-benefit analysis.' The two left-hand number columns refer to the K&U requirements for the alternative Diploma and NVQ assessment routes.

The text of the next three chapters also contain cross references to K&U items in the page margins.

The Business Environment			*page reference*
NVQ	*Diploma*		
1	1	The range of external regulations affecting accounting practice.	75-76
2	2	Common types of fraud.	76-79
3	3	The implications of fraud.	79-82

Management Techniques			
4	4	Methods for scheduling and planning work.	63-66
5	5	Techniques for managing your own time effectively.	61-62
6	6	Methods of measuring cost-effectiveness.	65-66
7	7	Methods of detecting fraud within accounting systems.	67,79-84
8	8	Techniques for influencing and negotiating with decision-makers and controllers of resources.	68-69
9	-	Techniques for reviewing recommendations through cost-benefit analysis	66-67

Management Principles and Theory			
10	9	Principles of supervision and delegation.	70-73
11	10	Principles of fostering effective working relationships, building teams and motivating staff.	70-73

The Organisation			
12	11	How the accounting systems of an organisation are affected by its organisational structure, its Management Information Systems, its administrative systems and procedures and the nature of its business transactions.	53-55
13	12	The overview of the organisation's business and its critical external relationships (customers/clients, suppliers, etc.).	51-52
14	13	The purpose, structure and organisation of the accounting function and its relationships with other functions within the organisation.	56-57
15	14	Who controls the supply of resources (equipment, materials, information and people) within the organisation.	58-59

Knowledge and Understanding evidenced in the Project

stages of the project   **K&U items which need evidencing**

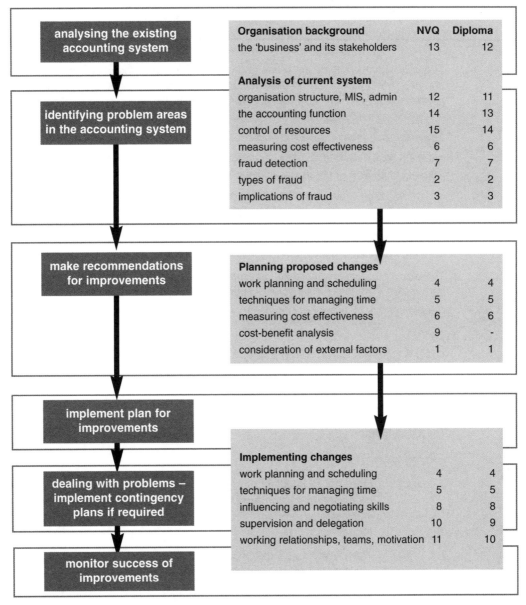

stages of the project	K&U items	NVQ	Diploma
analysing the existing accounting system	**Organisation background**		
	the 'business' and its stakeholders	13	12
identifying problem areas in the accounting system	**Analysis of current system**		
	organisation structure, MIS, admin	12	11
	the accounting function	14	13
	control of resources	15	14
	measuring cost effectiveness	6	6
	fraud detection	7	7
	types of fraud	2	2
	implications of fraud	3	3
make recommendations for improvements	**Planning proposed changes**		
	work planning and scheduling	4	4
	techniques for managing time	5	5
	measuring cost effectiveness	6	6
	cost-benefit analysis	9	-
	consideration of external factors	1	1
implement plan for improvements			
dealing with problems – implement contingency plans if required	**Implementing changes**		
	work planning and scheduling	4	4
	techniques for managing time	5	5
	influencing and negotiating skills	8	8
	supervision and delegation	10	9
monitor success of improvements	working relationships, teams, motivation	11	10

Notes:

- This diagram complements the checklist diagram on page 28 which maps the Performance Criteria to the Project stages.
- The wording of the Knowledge and Understanding items has been simplified here for ease of illustration.
- Note that K&U items 4, 5 and 6 can be evidenced in more than one part of the Project.

4 The organisation

this chapter covers . . .

In this chapter we examine the way in which the accounting function 'fits into' the overall structure of the organisation and how it relates to other organisations.

The chapter covers the main areas of the Knowledge and Understanding (K&U) which underlie 'The organisation' requirement of Unit 10. The relevant K&U items for the NVQ route and Diploma are covered and referenced in the page margins. The text also contains 'Project writing hints' which explain how the K&U theory should be evidenced.

The areas the chapter covers include:

- the type of business/areas of operation carried out by the organisation
- the influence of the external stakeholders of the organisation
- the overall structure of the organisation
- the structure of the accounting system
- the way in which the accounting system interacts with the other functions
- the administrative systems and control of resources within the organisation

You will see from these topics that this material forms much of what may well go into the introductory and analysis sections of your Project.

Supplementary questions to consolidate your learning follow on page 85.

KNOWLEDGE AND UNDERSTANDING COVERED

unit 10:
MANAGING SYSTEMS AND PEOPLE IN THE ACCOUNTING ENVIRONMENT

The Organisation

NVQ	Diploma	
12	11	How the accounting systems of an organisation are affected by its organisational structure, its Management Information Systems, its administrative systems and procedures and the nature of its business transactions.
13	12	The overview of the organisation's business and its critical external relationships (customers/clients, suppliers, etc.)
14	13	The purpose, structure and organisation of the accounting function and its relationships with other functions within the organisation.
15	14	Who controls the supply of resources (equipment, materials, information and people) within the organisation.

K&U:
NVQ 13
Diploma 12

THE 'BUSINESS' OF THE ORGANISATION

public and private sectors

Organisations are normally classed as private sector or public sector.

Public sector organisations are those owned or controlled directly or indirectly by the state. They include corporations like the BBC, Government Departments and local authorities. Their function is therefore largely to provide some form of service: broadcasting, health, education, policing, refuse collection, tax collection, for example. Some public sector organisations form partnerships with private sector companies to provide a service, eg some hospitals in the National Health Service.

Private sector organisations, on the other hand, are in private ownership, and include businesses ranging from the sole trader to the public limited company. The function of these organisations is to provide a product such a car or TV or a service such as a holiday or a foot massage.

The range of activities carried out by both public and private sector organisations – the nature of their 'business' can therefore be classified as:

* providing goods – either through manufacturing or through retailing
* providing a service – either for consumers (private sector) or as a social benefit (public sector)

You may not consider that tax collection is a social benefit, but if you appreciate that tax revenue is used for Government spending on health and education, you will see the logic, even though it hurts!

how the 'business' affects the accounting system

All organisations need accounting systems to carry out the accounting function. These functions include:

* processing and recording financial transactions – keeping accounts
* payroll
* costing and budgeting
* raising finance

You will see from this list that these are 'generic' functions which are common to all organisations. The variation is in the detail and will depend on the type of 'business' the organisation carries out:

* a manufacturing company in the private sector, for example, will keep accounts for suppliers and customers, will run payroll and will cost and budget for the manufacturing process and other activities; it is likely to raise finance from banks and possibly the equity markets

- a local authority in the public sector will keep accounts for suppliers and to a lesser extent for customers, it will run payroll and keep to strict budgets; its financing, however, will come from Central Government, local enterprises and from local taxation

> **Project writing hint**
>
> When you write about the accounting system of your chosen organisation in the 'Organisation Background' section you will need to relate the system's functions to the 'business' – the activity – of the organisation.

K&U:
NVQ 13
Diploma 12

DEALING WITH EXTERNAL STAKEHOLDERS

A stakeholder is a person or organisation that has an 'interest' in another organisation.

Stakeholders can be internal (eg employees, managers) or external (eg shareholders, banks, pressure groups). The Knowledge and Understanding requirement covers the relationship with the **external stakeholder**s of an organisation.

Take for example a retail organisation such as a supermarket chain run as a quoted public limited company. The functioning of the accounting system will be affected by external stakeholders in a number of ways:

- **shareholders** will require information about the financial performance of the company in the form of a printed financial statement or a similar document on the website

- **banks** that are lending money to the company are likely to require regular (eg monthly) management accounts, eg levels of sales, stock, cash held, creditors, debtors

- the **tax authorities** will require computation and payment of Corporation Tax, Value Added Tax and collection of Income Tax and National Insurance through the PAYE system

- **pressure groups** such as the health and environmental lobbies will affect costing and budgeting if more expensive suppliers have to be chosen because their products are 'greener' and more healthy

> **Project writing hint**
>
> When you write about the accounting system of your chosen organisation in the 'Organisation Background' section you will need to identify external stakeholders who place demands on the activities of the accounting system and possibly affect financial decisions.

K&U:
NVQ 12
Diploma 11

ORGANISATIONAL STRUCTURE

The organisation of the accounting system will depend a great deal on the way in which the organisation as a whole is structured – the **organisational structure**.

In the case of a smaller organisation such as a private company the structure will be based on the shareholder directors being in charge of the whole business, with possibly a finance director in charge of the finance and accounting function. The variation arises when the organisation is larger, in which case the structure is likely to be either

- a loosely organised group of independent operating units, directed by a managing company, or

- driven from the top and tightly controlled as a single unit

These are represented by the two basic types of organisational structure: flat and hierarchical.

flat structure

This is where operating divisions of an organisation are relatively independent, and are likely to have their own accounting systems. A typical example is where groups of companies are divided up in terms of geographical areas or products. It must be stressed that it will be the responsibility of the managing company to ensure that the accounting systems of the separate companies are harmonised and work together. Study the diagram below.

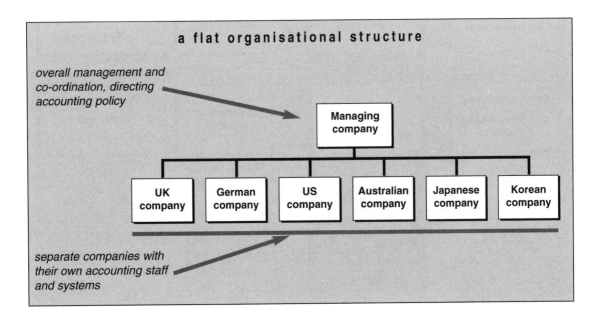

hierarchical structure

A hierarchy is a series of levels of people, each level controlled by the level above it. This structure – also known as a 'tall' structure – is suitable for a large organisation such as a public limited company or Government Department which may have thousands of employees. In this type of structure the accounting system will be the responsibility of the Finance Director and is centralised and strictly controlled. Study the diagram below.

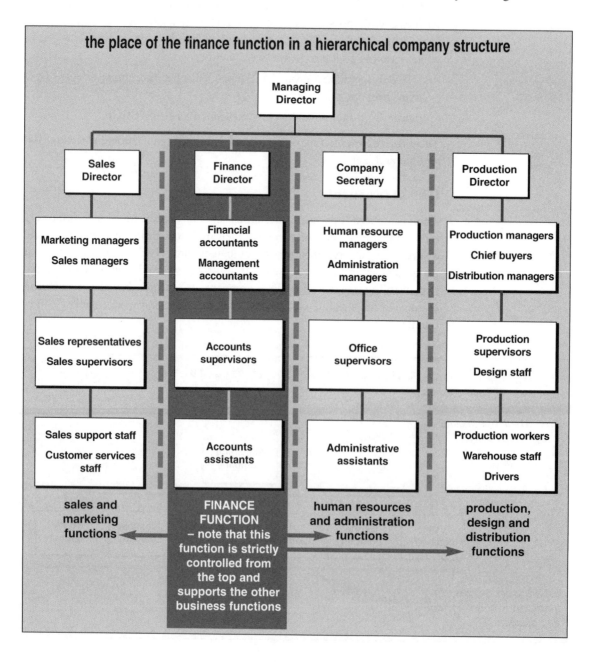

> **Project writing hint**
>
> When you write about the accounting system of your chosen organisation in the 'Analysis of Current System' section you will need to identify the type of organisational structure used as it may help to explain problems within the accounting system. For example, a flat structure may lead to lack of co-ordination between separate operating divisions and the use of different software; a hierarchical structure may lead to inflexibility, lack of job variety, lack of promotion and consequent demotivation.

**K&U:
NVQ 12
Diploma 11**

MANAGEMENT INFORMATION SYSTEMS (MIS)

A Management Information System (MIS) is precisely what it says it is: a computer-based system which provides up-to-date, accurate and relevant information to management. An efficient MIS will enable management to make informed decisions promptly. This will help the organisation achieve its objectives.

By 'management' we mean all levels of management, from line managers (supervisors) through to the Finance Director. Clearly the type and level of information required will vary according to the role of the manager and the type of decision expected from that manager.

Examples of the type of data produced by an accounting MIS include:

- sales figures for products and regions

- stock levels

- customer account details, ranging from balances to detailed reports such as the Aged Debtor Analysis

- budget reports showing variances

- profitability reports by product

You will see from this range of information that decision-making can range from 'Do we allow this customer any more credit?' through to 'Do we continue to manufacture this product?'

> **Project writing hint**
>
> When you write about the accounting system of your chosen organisation in the 'Analysis of Current System' section you will need to assess the MIS available. Does it enable management to make the required decisions? Is it communicated effectively within the accounting system? Can it be improved?

K&U:
NVQ 14
Diploma 13

ACCOUNTING SYSTEM: ORGANISATION AND STRUCTURE

The Project requires you to look critically at the existing accounting system and to identify areas for improvement in both the system itself and the way in which it is managed.

A typical accounting system carries out a number of functions, shown in the diagram below. It is the responsibility of the management to ensure that it operates smoothly.

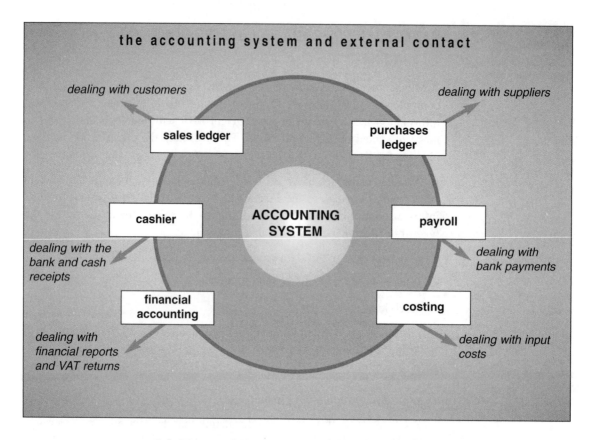

It is important that the accounting system is not seen to operate in isolation. Part of your requirement for this Knowledge and Understanding item is to analyse the way in which the accounting system integrates with the other internal functions of the organisation.

If the organisation is a manufacturing business, these other functions might include production, human resources, sales and marketing, administration.

Study the diagram on the next page to see how the accounting system inter-relates with some of the other internal functions of the organisation.

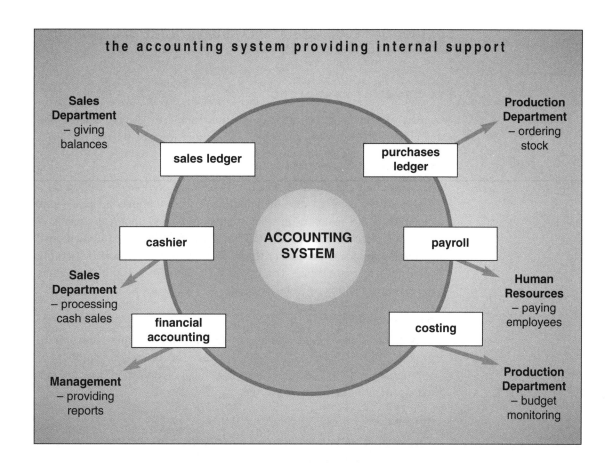

the accounting system providing internal support

Sales Department – giving balances

sales ledger

purchases ledger

Production Department – ordering stock

cashier

ACCOUNTING SYSTEM

payroll

Sales Department – processing cash sales

financial accounting

costing

Human Resources – paying employees

Management – providing reports

Production Department – budget monitoring

K&U 13

Project writing hint

When you write about the accounting system of your chosen organisation in the 'Analysis of Current System' section you will need to analyse the way in which the organisation structures its accounting system. Some form of structure chart would be a useful aid, and could be included within the Appendices.

The analysis might identify weaknesses in the way the system is structured, in the way it is managed and in the way in which it communicates with people – eg customers or suppliers – **outside** the organisation.

The analysis should also look at the way in which the accounting system deals with other functions **inside** the organisation. A good starting point is to look at communications between the various departments. Is the system at fault at all? Is there a management weakness?

CONTROL OF RESOURCES BY INDIVIDUALS IN THE ORGANISATION

the need for resources

Adequate resources are essential to the functioning of an organisation. All come at a cost. Resources can be classified under four main headings:

- **equipment and material resources**

  These include premises in which to work and equipment needed on a day-to-day basis. They also include the materials that may be used – raw materials, stock and consumables such as biros and photocopy paper. A car manufacturer will clearly have a greater need for equipment and material resources in a factory than a firm of insurance brokers working from a town centre office. The important point here is that in both cases the resources will need to be adequate.

- **human resources**

  This term is now used widely to describe the 'people' function in organisations. There is always a need for the right number of appropriately skilled people to work within an organisation, whether in a management or an operational role.

- **information**

  This is an essential resource and must be readily available to whoever needs it within the organisation. Computer-based systems with up-to-date and accurate information are the ideal solution. Information in a manufacturing or retail business, for example, will include product specifications, prices, stock levels, customer orders, supplier orders. A travel agency will need different types of information, but equally, the data will need to be accurate and up-to-date and on computer screen.

- **financial resources**

  This term means 'money' which is either available currently or can be made available within a set time period to allow spending in line with a particular budget allocation. This is probably the most critical type of resource for the functioning of the organisation. It affects all areas.

control of resources by individuals

This Knowledge and Understanding item (NVQ 15/ Diploma 14) requires you to examine the way in which individuals within the organisation control the supply of the various resources described above. Control of resources is normally dictated by the various levels of budget within an organisation. You will be familiar with the different types of budget from your other studies.

For example, the production or staffing budget of a business is likely to be decided upon at director level and the departmental budget will be the responsibility of the departmental manager. Line managers (supervisors) will also have decisions to make about control of resources – for example they may be given the power to allow staff to work overtime and to order small items of office equipment. Employees at assistant level will also have control of resources at a reduced level, for example ordering stationery items or tea and coffee for the rest room. It is all a question of level and scale.

The diagram below sets out the hierarchy of individuals who will make decisions about controlling resources and shows 'level and scale'.

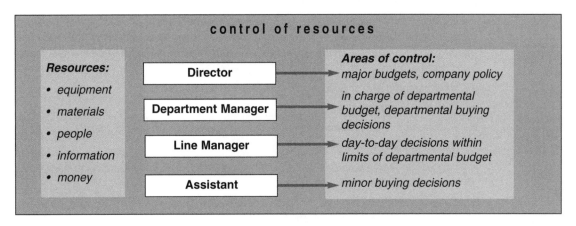

errors and fraud within the system

The control of resources brings with it the opportunity both for error and for fraud. Both can be avoided with the enforcement of checking and monitoring procedures. **Error** includes situations involving over-ordering of materials – for example ordering 5,000 suspension files instead of 100 where the units ordered were boxes of 50 rather than individual files. **Fraud** is a fact of life where control of resources is concerned. It can range from a director siphoning off funds by 'fiddling the books' to the supposedly innocent pilfering of biros and stationery at assistant level. The incidence of fraud is covered in detail in Chapter 6.

Note: K&U questions for this chapter follow in the section which starts on page 85.

K&U 14

Project writing hint

When you write about the accounting system of your chosen organisation in the 'Analysis of Current System' section you will need to identify the individuals who control resources, and comment on the scope of the purchasing decisions they can make and the control mechanisms that exist. You should look for areas in which efficiency in the control of resources and information provision could be improved. It would certainly not be diplomatic to carry out a major fraud investigation!

5 Management techniques and theory

In this chapter we start by describing the practicalities of managing work and people – the 'techniques' of management – and finish by discussing some of the theories which help to put these practicalities into perspective.

'Management techniques' comprises items 4 to 8 of the Knowledge and Understanding requirements of Unit 10 (both NVQ and Diploma). Many of these techniques will be needed when a change to the accounting system is proposed and implemented. The skills covered are:

- work planning and scheduling
- time management
- working out if recommendations are cost-effective, looking at cost-benefit analysis
- detecting fraud
- negotiation techniques used when dealing with decision makers and people who control resources

These issues are then put into theoretical perspective in relation to the Knowledge and Understanding requirements which deal with:

- supervision and delegation (NVQ 10 and Diploma 9)
- team building and motivation (NVQ 11 and Diploma 10)

KNOWLEDGE AND UNDERSTANDING COVERED

unit 10:
MANAGING SYSTEMS AND PEOPLE IN THE ACCOUNTING ENVIRONMENT

Management Techniques

NVQ	Diploma	
4	4	Methods for scheduling and planning work
5	5	Techniques for managing your own time effectively
6	6	Methods of measuring cost-effectiveness
7	7	Methods of detecting fraud within accounting systems
8	8	Techniques for influencing and negotiating with decision-makers and controllers of resources

Management Principles and Theory

NVQ	Diploma	
9	-	Techniques for reviewing recommendations through cost-benefit analysis
10	9	Principles of supervision and delegation
11	10	Principles of fostering effective working relationships, building teams and motivating staff

ORGANISING WORK AND MANAGING TIME

Whether you are a manager or an assistant, the organisation of your work requires a constant process of **planning** and **scheduling** tasks, reviewing progress and then planning and scheduling again. The work of an assistant is more likely to be dictated by set processes and a job description and the manager will be more involved in decision-making, negotiating and constantly reviewing priorities.

contingency planning

It is important for management to be able to deal with the unexpected event and anticipate it with some form of **contingency planning** . . . *'if this happens, then I will . . .'*. In contingency planning, a manager will need how to deal with emergencies such as computer breakdown, staff absences and sudden changes in work patterns.This may involve:

- asking staff to carry out tasks they are not used to doing
- asking staff to work extra hours
- taking on 'temp' staff

The manager must see to it that staff are well-trained, multi-skilled and motivated in order to cope with contingencies.

dealing with priorities

Day-to-day work involves a wide variety of tasks competing for time. The question 'what next?' involves identifying and prioritising tasks that need to be done.

There are a number of different types of task, in an accounts office . . .

- **routine tasks**

    These are everyday tasks such as reading the post and emails, checking invoices, inputting runs of data, sending standard letters, answering telephone queries, chasing overdue accounts. They do not hold any great surprises, but their efficient completion is important to the smooth running of the office.

- **non-routine tasks**

    These are the unexpected tasks such as helping with one-off projects, working out of the office on a special assignment, or helping to clear up after the washroom has flooded. These may hold up normal routine work.

Routine tasks are easy to plan for because they are predictable.

Non-routine tasks cannot be planned for, and they can sometimes cause problems, as we will see later in the chapter. They call for flexibility and logical thinking, skills which to some extent can be developed.

In addition, tasks may be **urgent** and they may be **important**. These are not always the same thing . . .

- **urgent tasks**

    These are tasks which have to be done by a specific pressing deadline: the Finance Director may need a spreadsheet immediately for a meeting currently taking place; customer statements may have to go out today.

- **important tasks**

    These are tasks for which the employee has been given personal responsibility. They may be part of the normal routine and other people depend on their successful completion, or they may have been delegated because the line manager thinks the employee is capable of them.

working out the priorities

Prioritising tasks means deciding in which order the tasks should be carried out. Which one first? Which one last? Which tasks matter? Which tasks do not matter so much?

The guide to the basic order of priority is shown below. You may, of course, think of exceptions to this rule, particularly with items 2 and 3.

an order of priority . . .

1 Tasks that are **urgent and important** – they have got to be done soon and if you do not do them you are going to let a lot of people down – eg producing the spreadsheet for the Finance Director's meeting.

2 Tasks that are **urgent but less important**, eg preparing statements for posting to customers – if the job is not completed today, the job still needs doing, but the business is not going to grind to a halt if the job is not done in the short term.

3 Tasks that are **important but not urgent**, eg producing some sales figures for a management meeting at the end of the week – the task has to be done, but it could be done tomorrow.

4 Tasks that are **neither important nor urgent**, eg archiving material from some old files. This task is a useful 'filler' when the work flow becomes less busy; it would not matter, however, if it were put off for a week or two.

K&U 4

PLANNING AIDS

'To Do' lists

Making lists of things 'to do' are very common both at work and at home. It is the organised person, however, who writes these lists on an ongoing basis, possibly daily, incorporating actions which have not been ticked off on the previous day in a new list. In other words, tasks that have not been done are carried forward onto a new list.

Lists may be written on paper or they may be compiled on the computer as a form of electronic 'Post-it' note. Managers implementing changes to an accounting system will inevitably need to prepare a daily list.

'To do' lists may be subdivided to show the priorities of the tasks to be done. Look at the example drawn up by a line manager below.

'TO DO' LIST   1 April

urgent stuff

1   Aged debtors schedules for the Accounts Manager for today.

2   Sales summaries for Costings section for today.

3   Get March statements in the post today.

non-urgent

1   Print out activity reports for overseas customers.

2   Set up spreadsheet for regional sales analysis.

3   Look into venues for staff evening out.

---

diaries

The diary organises tasks in terms of time. They are very useful planning aids and ensure – if they are efficiently kept – that tasks and events do not clash. Diaries can be paper-based or electronic. They can be individual diaries or office or 'section' diaries used for a group of employees.

The traditional paper-based diary with a week to view can be used alongside 'To do' lists as an efficient way of time planning and prioritising. Some people keep the 'To do' lists in their diary.

planning schedules

Planning schedules are more complex planning devices which deal with project situations – such as changes to an accounting system:

- some tasks *have to* follow on from each other – to give a simple example, you have to boil the water before making a cup of instant coffee – these are known as **critical** activities; you cannot achieve what you want without doing them in sequence

- some tasks are **non-critical** – they are important, but the timing is not so crucial – you will have to put instant coffee in the cup, but you can do it while the kettle is boiling or even the day before if you want!

Sometimes there will be a non-routine activity in the workplace, which is complicated and involves a number of inter-dependent tasks. Organisations often use a visual representation of the tasks in the form of horizontal bars set against a time scale to help with the planning. These are known as Gannt charts and can be drawn up manually, or, more often these days, on the computer screen using dedicated software.

action plans

After a series of activities has been scheduled over time, as in the example of the Gannt chart, the organisation can then carry out more detailed planning in the form of an **action plan** which will:

- define each activity in detail

- establish start dates for individual activities

- establish target finish dates

- state who is responsible for carrying out each activity

- in some cases state the budgeted cost of each activity

This type of plan is a form of checklist which can be regularly monitored and amended as required. Plans rarely go according 'to plan'. Computer spreadsheets are often used for setting out action plans because they can be easily amended and printed out in revised form.

the importance of monitoring

An important aspect of managing people and activities (such as the proposed change to the system) is **monitoring** what is going on. Is everything going to plan? If it is, tasks can be carried out in the decided order of priority. If it is not, changes will have to be made: tasks may change in order of priority, tasks may have to be delegated or delayed, or the manager may have to ask for help. This planning and monitoring process can be seen in the diagram at the top of the next page.

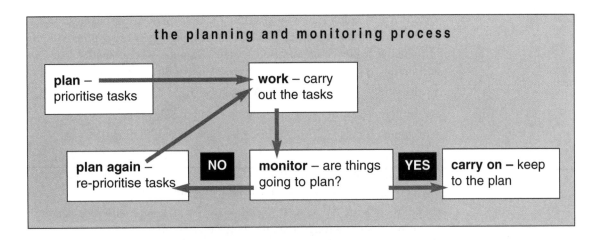

Project writing hint (K&U items 4 & 5)

When you write about the proposed change to the accounting system, you will need to look critically at the way in which the system is managed in terms of work planning and scheduling, and whether time is managed effectively. Are planning aids used? Are tasks prioritised? Are contingency plans in place? You will need to provide evidence that these management skills are being used. Note that evidence can also relate to the <u>implementation</u> of the change, using the same criteria.

K&U 6

MEASURING COST EFFECTIVENESS

what is cost effectiveness?

When assessing possible changes to an accounting system it is important to carry out an exercise which ensures that the organisation will be getting value for money.

Cost effectiveness means achieving the objectives set by the organisation in the most cost efficient way. In the case of the public sector this results in what is known as 'Best Value' and in the case of the private sector by the simple term 'profitability'.

measuring cost effectiveness

Managing cost effectiveness involves:

- setting targets using performance indicators
- setting a budget to achieve those targets
- setting up a system to monitor success in meeting targets

Take, for example, a company running a busy mail order business selling DVDs and computer games. It is planning to change its order processing by introducing a new computerised system. Targets – benchmarks – for the accounting system might include performance indicators such as:

- the number of sales orders processed per hour
- the percentage of errors in the processing of sales invoices
- the time it takes to process an order from receipt to despatch
- the number of orders which become bad debts through credit card 'chargebacks' (ie where the credit card company claims the money back again where the transaction is disputed by the customer)
- the quality of the system, eg the number of complaints received from customers (eg wrong price, discounts missed off)

The ultimate objective of this new system will be to increase the number of orders received because of the increased efficiency of the service and the better feedback from customers about service quality.

monitoring cost-effectiveness

As well as setting a budget for this new system, the accounting function must set up a system for regularly monitoring cost effectiveness through these performance indicators using both internal data and also external data such as customer surveys of service quality. Management must be able to review the performance indicators, examine any variances against the departmental budget, and take remedial action if the need arises.

Project writing hint

Knowledge & Understanding requirement 6 requires you to provide evidence of the measurement of cost-effectiveness of the proposed change(s) in the accounting system. The evidence does not need to be a full financial projection, but details of performance indicators required and the monitoring arrangements will suffice. This evidence also relates to Performance Criterion 10.2C.

K&U: NVQ 9

COST-BENEFIT ANALYSIS

Cost-benefit analysis compares the amount of resources used with the benefits obtained from a project.

using cost-benefit analysis

Cost-benefit analysis can be used to measure the financial outcome of a project. In order to do this the cash flow generated by a project needs to be quantified. This should be done by:

1 identifying the cash inflows (this may include cash savings)

2 identifying the cash outflows for each year

3 subjecting the difference between the cash inflow and outflow for each year to discounted cash flow techniques

Some organisations may also use the payback technique by identifying how quickly a project pays back the original capital investment in a project.

It is also important to appreciate that there may be some benefits from a project that cannot be measured in financial terms, for example:

* better communication links between staff

* an improvement in the quality of a service provided

* a more effective reporting system

These benefits should be included in the assessment of your project.

Project writing hint

When you make a recommendation in respect of a project you can use cost-benefit analysis to identify its financial outcome. You can use a positive financial outcome to support your recommendations.

K&U 7

DETECTING FRAUD

An important responsibility of any manager is the detection of fraud within the accounting system. This topic is covered in full in the next chapter 'Dealing with fraud'. Knowledge and Understanding item 7 'Methods of detecting fraud within accounting systems' highlights the managerial role of policing the accounting system. The manager must develop the detective skills of sensing anything unusual about employees and transactions. It may, of course, be the case that the fraud is taking place at a higher level in the organisation; in this situation the manager should become a 'whistle blower'.

Project writing hint

The subject of fraud is covered in full in the next chapter and also in the evidence produced for Performance Criteria 10.2.B 'Identify potential areas of fraud arising from control avoidance within the accounting system and grade the risk'. The Knowledge and Understanding requirement (item 7) stresses the managerial role of fraud detection and the evidence produced must relate to this managerial technique.

NEGOTIATING WITH DECISION MAKERS AND STAFF

Two important inter-related management techniques are influencing and negotiating – the art of persuading people around to a particular point of view. In the case of your Project there is the need to persuade the organisation to accept your proposal for a change in the accounting system.

The people that will need to be persuaded are

- senior managers and directors – the decision makers and controllers of resources (ie of staff, funding, premises and equipment)

and if the proposal is accepted . . .

- other employees who will be affected by the change

influencing and negotiating skills

How do managers influence and persuade other people to do what they want them to do? Firstly, some key principles need to be understood . . .

we all have different personalities

Having different personalities usually means we also have differing viewpoints on many things. Poor managers try to get people to do things without really understanding this simple truth. They forget that people need consulting and talking to politely and reasonably. Instead they try to change things in a rush, making people more hostile to the proposed changes than they might have been in the first place.

we all see the same situations differently

For example, a manager might want to change the layout of a large open plan office. The manager will perceive this as a way of increasing working efficiency. However, individual staff will perceive these changes in all sorts of ways:

- If they are relocated to different parts of the office some staff may feel offended – perhaps they will lose their window seat or they may get a smaller desk or a smaller working area or a more noisy area. They may have been put next to somebody they cannot stand!

- Others may perceive the changes as an omen of something far worse: potential job losses, perhaps.

The unforeseen consequences could include some good employees making the decision to look for a new job.

All these perceptions have arisen because managers have not tried to persuade people that the changes in room layout are a good idea!

the ways in which managers influence people

To avoid the kinds of mistakes illustrated above, managers should use a variety of techniques and approaches to influence people. Managers should be ready to use a variety of approaches; these will depend on the circumstances of each situation. These techniques and approaches include:

- managers must give reasons for their decisions and be upfront about it

- managers should adopt a friendly approach when dealing with people; unpleasantness gets nobody anywhere

- managers should get the support of a few people so they can use this as leverage over the rest

- managers should bargain for people's support . . .

  "do this for me and I will do this for you...."

- sometimes managers have to be assertive or 'heavy' with people, but this should never mean being aggressive or unpleasant

- managers will use the weight of more senior colleagues to persuade people to go along with their plans; a typical comment might be

  "I know that the Managing Director will go along with my plan"

the use of negotiating skills by managers

Negotiation is another key technique which involves influencing people. Examples include:

- negotiation of a contract with another organisation to supply raw materials

- negotiation with a potential employee on the terms and conditions of employment

To negotiate effectively managers must ensure that they:

- prepare their case properly

- are clear about what they aim to achieve

- work out their tactics and strategy

- know which areas they are prepared to negotiate over and in which areas they are not prepared to compromise under any circumstances

> **Project writing hint**
>
> The Project should provide evidence that the management skills of influencing and negotiating have been used in persuading the organisation to adopt the improvement in the accounting system. This could include records of meetings and discussions with employees of the organisation and notes relating to the outcomes achieved.

SUPERVISION, TEAM-WORKING, DELEGATION, AND MOTIVATION

principles of supervision and teamwork

Effective supervision, like the skill of influencing, is a key management role in any organisation. The key principles of good supervision are:

organise work so that employees get the most out of it

Work should be as appropriate as possible for the person being asked to do it, a factor sometimes forgotten by managers. The key thing here is that people should do what they are good at and what they like to do. This is not always easy to achieve but the consequences of doing this are:

- a contented workforce
- better quality work
- low staff turnover

create the best possible conditions for employees

This means consulting employees to find out what they want. In the last section (page 68) we saw the outcome of management not consulting people about a change in the room layout.

create a team that will work well together

This means creating good team spirit and high morale. Sometimes managers will take their employees on team building weekends to encourage them to work better together. It has to be said that these kinds of weekends can have very mixed results!

Creating a team means:

- selecting the right staff to work together
- making the most of the individual strengths in the team
- handing out work fairly to team members
- giving members of the team opportunities for personal career development, eg allowing them to study for AAT qualifications
- monitoring team members' progression in the organisation through a proper system of appraisals
- consulting with them to get their views on a wide range of issues
- giving them credit for their contribution and ideas
- being fair and impartial in the way that team members are treated

supporting employees

Managers should support employees on a day-to-day basis – giving them back-up to ensure that they have the right resources and that they feel valued.

principles of delegation

Managers should be good at delegating. 'Delegation' is the situation where a manager gives responsibility to more junior employees. It may mean giving them a specific job to do, to be completed within a specific time period. More commonly it means giving employees the scope and authority to take on a more responsible role, sometimes for long periods of time.

If a manager delegates, he or she must be willing to delegate the authority as well as the responsibility. In an accounting context, this might mean giving a more junior employee the authority to sign cheques or to approve increases in credit limits within certain parameters.

If the manager delegates well, employees get real opportunities for career development and acquire new skills as 'managers of the future.' An advantage to the manager is that delegation can relieve some of the day-to-day stresses and pressures of routine management.

delegation plan

It is important when a manager delegates that the exercise is carried out in an organised way and that a 'delegation plan' is drawn up. This will cover:

- the areas of responsibility that are delegated
- the resources – eg time and training – that will be made available to help the employee who is taking on the responsibility
- review points – periods of time – eg three and six months – after which the manager and the employee can review progress, discuss problems and plan the way ahead

motivating employees

People need to be motivated in order to work well. Effective motivation of employees means providing them with:

- elements of challenge
- potential for self development – opportunities to 'get on'
- work with variety in it
- the chance to make some decisions of their own
- the chance of social contact with colleagues
- a feeling that their job is of real value

The following are usually good indicators that motivation is *lacking* in a workplace: high levels of absenteeism, long tea breaks and long toilet breaks, poor quality of work, reluctance to work, employees looking for jobs elsewhere.

some motivation theories

You need to be aware of the theories of the key writers on motivation.

One of the best known is **Abraham Maslow (1908-1970)**. His view was that all employee motivation is about satisfying unsatisfied needs. He stated that there was a ranking of needs which must be achieved in the correct order – from the bottom to the top of a 'pyramid' (see diagram below). Basic physiological needs (eg food, water) are at the bottom and self actualisation is at the top.

the need . . .	which is achieved by . . .
self actualisation	personal growth and self fulfilment
Esteem	Recognition
	Achievement
	Status
Social needs	Affection/love/friendship
Safety needs	Security
	Freedom from pain and threats
Physiological needs	Food, water, fresh air

Once one need is satisfied it ceases to motivate and the next higher need 'up the pyramid' comes into play. This implies that higher level needs have more value than the ones at the bottom. In order for an employee to achieve personal growth and self-fulfilment, therefore, a manager should ensure that as far as is practically possible all the physiological, safety, social and esteem needs of an employee are fulfilled.

Although Maslow wrote his study in 1953 it is interesting to see that a survey carried out in 2003 showed that the main motivators for most people are still very similar:

safety and security	employees do not like being made redundant
good pay	important for physiological needs
affiliation	having sociable people to work with
career prospects	job advancement in an increasingly mobile workforce
work/life balance	combining work and the chance to have a social life – 'working to live' rather than 'living to work'

Other authors include:

Douglas McGregor (1906-64)

His theory was that managers manage their organisations using a theory X or a theory Y approach. Theory X assumes that employees are only extrinsically motivated, ie they are not motivated by their work, but only by what they get from it eg pay, holidays, short hours etc. The conclusion is that such employees need constant supervision and their work needs checking regularly to make sure that it is of the required standard.

Theory Y takes what might be called an optimistic view of employees. They are interested in what they do. They are said to be intrinsically motivated – they respond to new ideas from their manager, they work hard with little supervision and they do not continually need to be told what to do.

Frederick Herzberg (born 1923)

Herzberg's theory is based on the idea that certain parts of a job motivate people to work hard – these parts are called **satisfiers**. Without them employees will not be motivated to work hard. Examples of satisfiers are achievement, responsibility, the nature of the work itself.

Other areas of the job involve **hygiene factors**. These are essential parts of the job, but they do not motivate people. However, without them the satisfiers will not be effective. Examples include pay, working conditions, job security, a pension.

An example of how they link together is . . .

Suppose you have an interesting job that is very stimulating and gives you a real sense of achievement every day. However, the pay is not enough to provide a decent living standard and there is no pension scheme. The place where you work is in a run-down building in a run-down part of town. These hygiene factors will make it unattractive and, finally, demotivating.

This illustrates the reason why people in very interesting poorly paid jobs may give them up for less interesting better paid ones.

Note: K&U questions for this chapter follow in the section which starts on page 85.

Project writing hint

The Project should provide evidence that the management skills of supervision, delegation, fostering working relationships, team building and motivating have been in action in the implementation of the improvement in the accounting system. This could include records of situations, meetings and discussions involving the employees of the organisation, noting the outcomes achieved. References to management theories could be made where appropriate.

6 External regulation and dealing with fraud

this chapter covers . . .

This chapter starts by dealing with the external regulations that affect accounting practice. Some of these are required by legislation and affect areas such as taxation, auditing and the regulation of limited companies. Others are 'accounting standards' set both in the UK and internationally by independent accounting standards bodies.

The main part of the chapter explains the different types of fraud that can be committed within an organisation and discusses the implications of fraud:

- *assessing the risk of fraud occurring within an organisation*
- *identifying areas vulnerable to fraud*
- *designing the system so that fraud is minimised*
- *monitoring the system to ensure that fraud can be detected*
- *dealing with cases of fraud as appropriate*

KNOWLEDGE AND UNDERSTANDING COVERED

unit 10:
MANAGING SYSTEMS AND PEOPLE IN THE ACCOUNTING ENVIRONMENT

The Business Environment

1   *The range of external regulations affecting accounting practice.*

2   *Common types of fraud.*

3   *The implications of fraud.*

Management Techniques

7   *Methods of detecting fraud within accounting systems.*

K&U 1

EXTERNAL REGULATIONS AFFECTING ACCOUNTING PRACTICE

legislation

The term 'legislation' covers a wide range of regulations based on UK Acts of Parliament and European Directives. Organisations are affected by a number of legal regulations affecting the way in which an accounting system operates. Examples include:

- **taxation regulations** – affecting areas such as:
    - PAYE for individuals on the payroll: income tax, National Insurance and other deductions
    - Value Added Tax: VAT returns, invoice format, rates applied
    - corporation tax paid by limited companies

- **company law** – set out in the Companies Act 1985 – requires that company accounts (of larger companies) should be audited; financial statements are to be drawn up in a set format and sent to shareholders; larger companies have to provide copies of these accounts to Companies House where they can be inspected by the public

- **data protection law** – set out in the Data Protection Act 1998 – protects data (including financial data) relating to individual customers

- **late payment law** – set out in the Late Payment of Commercial Debt (Interest) Act 1998 – allows suppliers to charge interest on late payment of invoices

UK and international accounting standards

The **Financial Reporting Council** (FRC) is a unified, independent regulator which:

- sets, monitors and enforces accounting and auditing standards
- oversees the regulatory activities of the professional accountancy bodies
- regulates audit
- promotes high standards of internal regulation within companies ('corporate governance')

The membership of the Council includes wide and balanced representation at the highest levels from the business, investor, professional and other communities interested in corporate reporting and governance.

The FRC promotes good financial reporting through its subsidiary boards, which include the **Accounting Standards Board** (ASB), the **Financial Reporting Review Panel** (FRRP) and the **Auditing Practices Board**.

The FRC now takes a more active role in relation to the internal regulation of companies, ensuring that they comply with company law, accounting standards, and auditing standards.

Accounting standards have been developed by the **Accounting Standards Board,** a subsidiary board of the FRC to provide the rules, or framework, of accounting. The intention has been to reduce the variety of alternative accounting treatments. This framework for accounting is represented by **Statements of Standard Accounting Practice** (SSAPs) and **Financial Reporting Standards** (FRSs). You should be familiar with these from your study of other Units.

As you will know from your other studies (specifically Unit 11), large companies in the European Union (including UK plcs) are required to prepare their final accounts in accordance with **International Financial Reporting Standards** (IFRSs).

K&U 1

Project writing hint

When you write about the proposed change to the accounting system of your chosen organisation you will need to provide evidence that it takes account of any change in external factors such as changes in the law (eg company regulation, tax rates) and changes in accounting standards. These external factors could be incorporated into your SWOT analysis, which is recommended by AAT in relation to Performance Criterion 10.2F (see page 39).

K&U 2

TYPES OF FRAUD

human nature?

Fraud is an unfortunate fact of life within organisations, and some would say it is part of human nature. It sometimes hits the headlines, as when a merchant banker's PA diverted over £1 million of her employer's funds into designer clothes, cars, speedboats, and general high living. Amazingly, this went undetected for a long time.

Another fraud which has now become legendary is the Robert Maxwell case in which company pension funds were raided to finance the publishing mogul's private spending.

But fraud is also taking biros and stationery or inflating a travel claim. This may not hit the headlines, but the principle remains the same – dishonesty.

It is the responsibility of the management of an organisation to:

- identify areas where the risk of fraud exists and to grade the seriousness of the risk in each case

- set up control systems involving all staff to alert management to possible occurrence of fraud

- monitor those control systems on a regular basis to ensure that they are working

- deal with any incidence of fraud in an appropriate way, whether it be a formal warning or calling in the police

These will be dealt with in the course of this chapter. First, however, it is important to define what we mean by 'fraud'.

some definitions

Fraud covers a variety of offences, but a general definition of fraud is:

the use of deception with the intention of obtaining an advantage, avoiding an obligation or causing loss to someone else or to an organisation

Fraud is a criminal activity and is covered in the UK by a number of laws:

theft	dishonestly taking someone else's property (Theft Act)
false accounting	dishonestly destroying, defacing, concealing or falsifying an accounting record for personal gain or to cause loss to someone else (Theft Act)
bribery and corruption	taking or giving a bribe that might influence the actions of others (Prevention of Corrupt Practices Acts)
deception	obtaining property, money, services or evading liability by deception (Theft Act)

In practical terms fraud is normally a combination of any of the following:

- **theft** of property or money or information (eg someone raiding the petty cash)

- **falsification** of records so that property or money is passed to the wrong person (eg someone 'fiddling' the payroll)

- **collusion** – ie a 'set-up' between an employee and someone else outside the organisation, eg false invoices sent in by an outsider for supplies that were never made and authorised and paid by the person 'on the inside'

examples of fraud

There are many examples of fraud which are made public. Students involved in the public sector would find it useful to look at the HM Treasury Fraud Reports, available as downloads from the website www.hm-treasury.gov.uk. These contain examples of fraud in local authorities and Government departments. Types of fraud in the private sector are very similar. The examples below have been adapted from cases reported by a leading insurance company.

REPORTED CASES OF FRAUD

Theft of fuel stocks – *Total Loss £25,000*

A local authority had their own fuel pumps for supplying their motor vehicles. The employee in charge stole fuel over a long period as the stock checks were inadequate.

Payroll fraud: fictitious employees – *Total Loss £10,000*

The manager of an industrial cleaning company invented bogus employees, put them on the payroll and then cashed their pay cheques.

Bank deposits: teeming and lading – *In 10 months a total of £7,000 was stolen.*

A clerk in charge of a sub post office stole cash receipts due to be paid into the local bank. This was covered up by delaying paying in at the bank and altering the paying-in slips relating to subsequent deposits. Stealing money received from one source and then using money received from other sources to cover it up is known as 'teeming and lading'.

Cheque printing machine – *Total Loss £25,000*

A ledger clerk responsible for making regular payment of rent for advertising was in charge of a machine that printed cheques. Numerous small cheques were made out by him for the correct amounts but payable to him. It was several months before complaints from creditors, (who had not received their cheques) were investigated and the fraud uncovered.

Collusion: stock control system – *Total Loss £1 million*

A well known national company was defrauded by two gangs of employees working at the same location. The losses involved collusion between warehousemen and drivers who used the spare capacity on vehicles to remove goods from the depot. False information was entered into the computerised stock control system and their activities were only discovered when the police reported finding large amounts of the particular product in the hands of third parties.

Collusion: fictitious sub-contractors – *Total Loss exceeded £500,000*

A major contractor with well established control systems to vet payments were the victims of fraud by a section supervisor in collusion with a computer operator. Cheques were made out to fictitious sub-contractors and despatched to private addresses.

K&U 3&7

RISK ASSESSMENT AND FRAUD

risk assessment – the role of management

Knowledge & Understanding item 7 requires that you establish methods of detecting fraud within the accounting system; item 3 requires an appreciation of the implications of what happens when fraud takes place. Assessment of **fraud risk** is part of the **risk assessment** process which is the responsibility of organisations in both the private and the public sectors.

In the case of limited companies (private sector), the Turnbull Report has stated that directors have responsibility for ensuring that risk management practices are established as part of an effective internal control system.

In the public sector the guiding document to fraud risk is HM Treasury's 'Managing the Risk of Fraud – a Guide for Managers' available as a download from www.hm-treasury.gov.uk

The assessment of risk generally by management follows a number of distinct stages. This process applies equally to the assessment of fraud risk:

- setting up a risk management group and identifying objectives
- identifying the areas of risk of fraud
- grading the scale of the risk in each case
- developing a strategy to manage that risk
- setting up systems to detect and deal with fraud, allocating responsibility
- getting the systems up and running
- monitoring the running of the system

the internal control system

A robust internal control system is essential if management is going to be able to detect and deal with fraud.

There are various techniques that can be used for making an internal control system 'fraud resistant':

- **fraud staff**

  Some very large organisations may appoint employees – eg ex-bank or ex-police staff – to work full-time on fraud prevention and detection.

- **management responsibility**

  Managers should be given specific areas of responsibility and answerability – eg sections of the Accounts Department – to ensure that fraud is kept to a minimum.

- **management supervision**

  Management – particularly line management – should supervise accounting activities on a regular basis. This involves overseeing and checking activities such as data entry to computers, making payments and payroll processing.

- **segregation of duties**

  The system should be set up so that duties which, when combined, could lead to fraud, are given to different people – ie they are segregated. For example, the cashier taking in cash for a business should ideally not be the same person who makes out the paying-in slip for the bank. The danger is that some of the cash may disappear into the cashier's pocket.

- **lock & key**

  Physical security – locking valuable items away – is a sure deterrent to theft. This does not only apply to cash: the tendency of items such as laptop computers and mobile phones to disappear has become a well-known and ever-increasing statistic.

- **authorisation**

  Some accounting activities may require authorisation by a nominated official. This ranges from the authorisation of petty cash, signing of cheques over a certain amount to the investing of liquid funds, eg placing £250,000 on a money market account. Clearly the larger the amount, the more senior the person giving authorisation.

detecting fraud

We have already seen the various areas in which fraud can occur. Fraud can be detected by the experienced manager by simple observation and through experience. Some of the tell-tale and danger signs include:

- employees acting suspiciously – looking shifty and hiding paperwork

- employees with higher levels of spending than you would expect from their income – the payroll clerk who has a new Porsche
- employees working long hours and taking less than the normal holiday entitlement – it is often when employees are away that other employees notice suspicious signs and uncover criminal activity
- employees who have a grudge against the organisation – they may have been passed over for promotion or they may even have a political or ethical axe to grind
- employees who are known to be short of money – they may be struggling with a high mortgage or may even have a drugs problem

grading likelihood and impact

Part of the process of the management of fraud risk is the decision about whether a risk is a **likely** one or not. The likelihood of risk can be divided into three levels:

- **high** – the likelihood of fraud is at a high level (disappearing biros)
- **moderate** – the likelihood is possible (theft of cash, collusion)
- **low** – the likelihood is remote (removal of assets from a company pension fund)

Risk assessment also needs to decide whether the **impact** of the fraud is significant.

Impact can relate to the **financial state** of the organisation. A major loss through fraud could seriously affect profit and liquidity. For example, the fraudulent trading by an employee of Barings Bank led to its collapse. The fraud can also seriously affect employees, as in the Robert Maxwell case in which employees' pensions were appropriated by the Chairman and Chief Executive.

Generally speaking, frauds that are likely (the disappearing biro) have a lower impact than the remote risk (removal of assets from a company pension fund). The **impact** of a fraud can therefore be similarly graded:

- **high** – the effects of fraud are very serious for the organisation (Barings Bank, Robert Maxwell)
- **moderate** – the effects of the fraud are significant but can be dealt with internally, or in some cases by the police (theft, collusion)
- **low** – the impact of the fraud is insignificant (petty pilfering)

using a matrix to grade fraud risk

Organisations sometimes use a matrix to assess the extent of fraud risk in an accounting system. The areas of the system in which the fraud might occur must first be identified, for example:

- cash payments
- cash receipts
- sales ledger
- purchases ledger
- expenses
- stock control
- payroll
- fixed asset purchase

A matrix (or a section of a matrix) will then be drawn up for each of the areas identified. An example of entries in a typical matrix is illustrated below. The matrix might display:

- the identified risk area of the organisation
- the details of the type of fraud
- the role of the employee who may become involved in it
- any third party who may become involved through collusion
- the likelihood of the fraud (high, moderate, low)
- the impact of the fraud (high, moderate, low)

This matrix will then become a valuable tool which will enable management to assess the risks and establish an appropriate strategy for minimising them. Note that the format of the matrices you will encounter in your studies may vary. The example below is fairly typical and could be used in your Project.

accounting system fraud matrix – some sample entries

Details of Risk	Employees	Collusion	Likelihood	Impact
Payroll section: Stationery pilferage	payroll staff	none	high	low
Theft of cash	payroll staff	none	moderate	moderate
Payments to fictitious employees	payroll staff	third party recipients	moderate	moderate
Purchase ledger: Paying fictitious suppliers	buyer	third party recipients	moderate	moderate
etc . . . etc . . .				

K&U 3&7

Project writing hint

The AAT recommends that in order to generate evidence for Performance Criterion 10.2B you should not only research into potential areas of fraud, but you should also identify each type of fraud and grade its impact, using some form of matrix – such as the one on the previous page. This will also contribute to the evidence for Knowledge & Understanding items 3 and 7. Remember, however, that you will need to be diplomatic with the organisation that you are dealing with, as fraud is a very sensitive issue.

K&U 7

FRAUD POLICY

Knowledge & Understanding item 7 asks for evidence of methods of fraud detection. We have already seen on pages 79 and 81 some of the warning signs of fraud which managers should look out for as a matter of course. It is useful, however, for an organisation to set up a **Fraud Policy** which might include:

- a clear indication of which managers are responsible for which potential areas of fraud and at what levels

- setting up of control systems to help avoid fraud, eg strict checking, segregation of tasks and division of responsibilities, eg in the purchasing process the person who sets up a purchase order should not be the same as the person who approves it or the person who writes out cheques should not be the same person who signs it (unless maybe it is for a very small amount)

- the regular monitoring of the control systems to ensure that they are working satisfactorily and are amended from time-to-time as circumstances require

- decisions about which type of frauds are significant (eg moderate and high risk) and should be acted upon and those which should be generally guarded against but which are low risk and do not require strict disciplinary action (eg the 'borrowed' biro) – see pages 80 to 81

- the need for an anti-fraud 'culture', ie instilling in employees the notion that any form of fraud (including the 'borrowed' biro) is inherently wrong and alerting them to the risks that exist

- following on from the last point, the mechanism should exist for 'whistle-blowing', ie for employees to alert the management if they become aware of any fraudulent goings-on at any level of the organisation; the employee in this case is given protection by the Public Interest Disclosure Act 1998

action taken to deal with fraud

As part of its Fraud Policy, an organisation should set up a system which ensures that the correct action is taken when:

- fraud is discovered by someone within the organisation
- fraud is reported by someone outside the organisation – the police, for example

Areas which should be dealt with are:

- provision of clear directions to managers about whom to contact when a fraud is discovered
- in a large organisation the appointment of a senior manager with special responsibility for fraud who can take responsibility for any major occurrences
- directions for disciplinary procedures for occurrences of fraud which will not have to involve the police and possible prosecution
- directions for how to deal with a case of fraud which will involve the notification of the police and may result in a criminal prosecution
- directions for how to deal with a case of fraud which is reported to the organisation by the police (eg the discovery of stolen stock or a bank reporting suspicious money transactions) – and which may result in a criminal prosecution

As you will have gathered from this chapter, fraud is inevitable. The lesson for the organisation is – be prepared.

Project writing hint   **K&U 7**

Knowledge & Understanding item 7 requires that you provide evidence of the organisation's 'methods of fraud detection'. These should include a note of any formal Fraud Policy, and if this does not exist, details of managerial control systems and any arrangements made for these systems to be monitored. Evidence of the introduction of any anti-fraud culture could also be included.

---

some useful websites

www.sfo.gov.uk

www.icaew.co.uk

www.hm-treasury.gov.uk.

In order to access information about fraud you may have to carry out a site search on 'fraud'. You may find www.scambusters.com a US site, also worth a visit.

Note: K&U questions for this chapter follow in the section which starts on page 85.

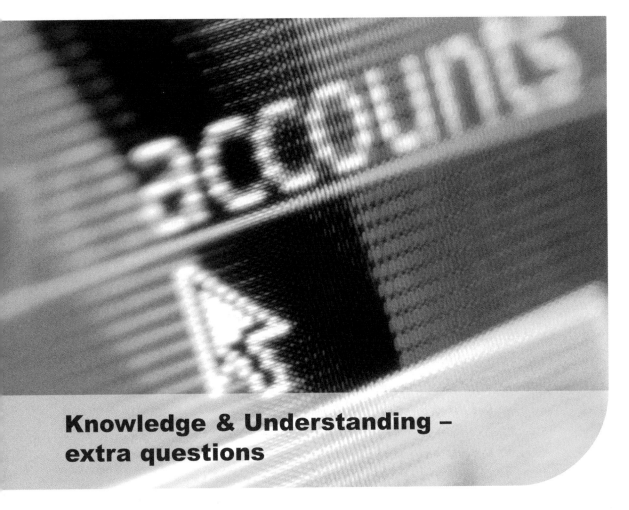

Knowledge & Understanding – extra questions

Section 3 concludes with a series of questions based on the Knowledge & Understanding requirements of Unit 10.

A list of the Knowledge & Understanding items is set out on the next page and the questions are presented in a sequence following the order of those items.

The numbering system for the questions is based on the K&U item numbers, ie each question number is prefixed by the appropriate K&U item number.

Note that because the NVQ qualification has an extra K&U item (number 9) there is a dual numbering system for the K&U of NVQ and Diploma routes after item 8.

Tutor notes on the questions are available to tutors direct from Osborne Books on request (please telephone 01905 748071 for terms and conditions of issue).

Knowledge & Understanding

The full Knowledge and Understanding (K&U) requirements of Unit 10 are set out below.

Students taking the NVQ assessment route should note that a new K&U requirement 9 has been added: 'Techniques for reviewing recommendations through cost-benefit analysis.' The two left-hand number columns refer to the K&U requirements for the alternative Diploma and NVQ assessment routes.

The Business Environment

NVQ	Diploma	
1	1	The range of external regulations affecting accounting practice.
2	2	Common types of fraud.
3	3	The implications of fraud.

Management Techniques

4	4	Methods for scheduling and planning work.
5	5	Techniques for managing your own time effectively.
6	6	Methods of measuring cost-effectiveness.
7	7	Methods of detecting fraud within accounting systems.
8	8	Techniques for influencing and negotiating with decision-makers and controllers of resources.
9	-	Techniques for reviewing recommendations through cost-benefit analysis

Management Principles and Theory

10	9	Principles of supervision and delegation.
11	10	Principles of fostering effective working relationships, building teams and motivating staff.

The Organisation

12	11	How the accounting systems of an organisation are affected by its organisational structure, its Management Information Systems, its administrative systems and procedures and the nature of its business transactions.
13	12	The overview of the organisation's business and its critical external relationships (customers/clients, suppliers, etc.).
14	13	The purpose, structure and organisation of the accounting function and its relationships with other functions within the organisation.
15	14	Who controls the supply of resources (equipment, materials, information and people) within the organisation.

K&U 1

The range of external regulations affecting accounting practice

Pages 75-76 in the textbook

1.1 The Chancellor of the Exchequer's annual budget can have significant influence on some of the operations carried out by the accounting function of a business organisation.

List three areas where changes announced in the Budget might affect an organisation's accounting and explain what those changes might be.

1.2 A firm of solicitors is contemplating changing its status from a partnership to a limited company. What additional activities will need to be carried out to comply with the requirements of the Companies Act?

1.3 What influence does the Accounting Standards Board have over the operation of the accounting function of business organisations?

K&U 2

Common types of fraud

Pages 76-79 in the textbook

You are investigating the accounting system of a building wholesaler that sells for cash over the counter and on credit to customers. You come across the following practices which raise your suspicions. In each case state what type of fraud may be involved and explain how it works and is often covered up.

2.1   You notice that although cash is regularly received over the trade counter, there is some considerable delay in paying it in at the bank. You also see that the cashier is also the person who completes the paying-in slip and there is no control system in place to check the figures on the paying-in slip.

2.2   You notice that the accounts office has only one printer used for printing invoices, credit notes and other financial documents. You also see that the office seems to get through at least three printer cartridges a week, judging by the deliveries that are received.

2.3   You are looking through the computerised payroll report for the last few weeks' wages. You notice that there are regular cash payments to employees described as 'casual workers'. You have not encountered any of these workers in your work in the office. The employee in charge of payroll, who inputs the details on the computer and looks after the cash says "Oh yes, they come and go, but we still have to put them on the payroll for PAYE purposes."

2.4   You are discussing customers with the line manager who looks after the purchases ledger. You have noticed that one supplier in particular charges much more for paving slabs than you would normally expect. You ask "Do you get quotes in for these slabs, they seem rather expensive?" The reply comes "No – I have known the supplier for years – there's no problem there."

K&U 3

The implications of fraud

Pages 79-82 in the textbook

3.1   One of the implications of fraud is that an organisation has to appreciate that

• some frauds are more likely than others

• some frauds have more impact than others

This means that some form of fraud risk assessment has to take place.

The business you are investigating has graded risks into three levels: 'high, medium and low'. You are to assess the potential risks listed and complete the matrix shown below, adding if there is any possible collusion with outsiders, stating who they might be.

details of potential fraud	collusion with outsiders	likelihood	impact of risk
theft of stationery			
fictitious suppliers on purchase ledger			
theft of investment funds from company portfolio			

3.2   You are investigating a large company finance department. During the course of the financial year the following frauds have been uncovered:

(a)   £1,250 loss through pilferage of stock in the warehouse (the stock has not been recovered)

(b)   £5,000 loss through overpayment of supplier invoices (the supplier is now bankrupt)

(c)   £150,000 taken from the employees' pension fund by director who has subsequently been killed in a sky diving accident. The Trustees of the pension fund are claiming the money back from the company by holding the company liable for the fraud of its director.

You are to state in each case the impact of these frauds on the <u>financial state</u> of the company.

K & U 4

Methods for scheduling and planning work

Pages 63-65 in the textbook

4.1 You are working in a fully computerised accounts office which has five staff carrying out the normal accounting functions.

What aids to scheduling and planning day-to-day routine work are likely to be used by that office?

4.2 You work in a management role in a large company which is planning a major reorganisation of its accounting function. This will involve relocation of the offices within the building, the purchase of new computer equipment and staff retraining.

(a) What planning aid might you use to ensure that all the required tasks are completed in sequence and on time? Describe briefly how it works.

(b) What planning aid might you use to provide more detailed planning, allocating responsibilities to individuals and possibly incorporating budget figures. Describe briefly how it works.

4.3 Contingency planning (planning for the unexpected events) is an important management technique. What measures would you take to prepare for the following situations:

(a) A major crash of the computer system used for entering ledger transactions and payroll.

(b) A vicious virus which results in 50% of employees being off sick.

(c) A sudden rush in sales orders which results in a 100% increase in volume of invoicing on the computers.

K&U 5

Techniques for managing your own time effectively

Pages 61-62 in the textbook

5.1 The ten tasks below are examples of activities which a payroll assistant may have to carry out in an Accounts Department of a medium-sized company. It is Monday in the last week of the month and the office has just opened. Employees in the organisation are paid monthly, on the last day of the month, which is at the end of this week. The payroll has to be run through the computer on Monday and BACS instructions sent to the bank on Tuesday so that employees can be paid on Friday.

Reorganise the list, placing the tasks in order of priority.

■   Look at the diary and compare with your 'To Do' list.

■   Send email to Marketing Department asking for monthly overtime figures to be sent through – they should have been received last Friday.

■   Check that details of hours worked (including overtime) have been received from all departments.

■   Draw up a notice advertising a staff trip out for next month.

■   Process the hours of all the employees on the computer. Print out pay details and a payroll summary, including the schedule setting out the amount which will have to be paid to the HM Revenue & Customs for income tax and National Insurance Contributions by 19th of the next month.

■   Pass the payroll printouts to your line manager for checking, and when approved, print out the payslips for distribution.

■   Put a note in the diary for the HM Revenue & Customs cheque to be prepared on 5th of next month.

■   Print out payroll statistics from the computer for your line manager – they are required for next week.

■   Prepare the BACS payroll schedule for the bank to process on Tuesday.

■   Pass the BACS payroll schedule to your line manager for checking.

K&U 6

Methods of measuring cost-effectiveness

Pages 65-66 in the text

6.1   You are investigating a small business which employs five people and is owned by Emma Zaphim. At present the accounting system is run on a manual basis: all the ledgers are written up by hand, the invoices, credit notes and statements are typed out and the payroll is worked out on Inland Revenue deduction sheets. There is a computer in the office which is used for correspondence and online connection. The owner is considering computerising the accounts and payroll using 'off-the-shelf' packages. She asks "how do I know it will be worth it and that I will get my money back?".

You suggest carrying out a cost-effectiveness exercise.

Task

Explain to Emma what a cost-effectiveness exercise will involve and what information you will need from her in order to carry out the exercise.

6.2   Alpha plc sells financial services such as investments and pensions through a UK network of sales reps. The board has recently decided to increase its presence in the market following a relaxation in the selling regulations. Alpha has received a proposition from Phoenix Systems, a company which operates telephone call centres based in the UK and overseas to expand its telesales operations. This will complement the efforts of the existing and very successful travelling sales force.

Phoenix Systems has stressed to Alpha plc the savings that will be made by outsourcing the telesales, but the board of Alpha is very concerned about its profitability and getting value for money.

Task

Describe how Alpha plc might assess the cost-effectiveness of this proposition.

K&U 7

Methods of detecting fraud within accounting systems

Pages 67 and 79-83 in the text

7.1 You are a management consultant and have been called in by Dodgee Systems to sort out its accounting system. The company has recently experienced a spate of fraud, including theft of cash, fiddling of wage payments and collusion with a supplier by someone working in the Purchase Ledger.

The company at present has no Fraud Policy.

Task

Describe the recommendations you would make to establish a formal system of control and fraud detection within the accounting system of Dodgee Systems.

7.2 You are having a coffee with a friend who works in the Finance Department of Lacey Fair Council, a local authority. She says "Guess what? One of the accounts line managers has been in trouble for getting hold of a whole load of names and addresses on computer file and selling them for some fantastic sum to someone in the marketing business. Mind you, all sorts of things go on in the Department – some computer laptops and a projector went for a walk the other day and nothing much seems to have been done about it. People seem to ignore what is going on!"

Task

Explain what may be going wrong at Lacey Fair Council. What criminal offences have been committed? What could be done by the management to help to prevent and detect fraud?

K&U 8

Techniques for influencing and negotiating with decision-makers and controllers of resources

Pages 68-69 in the text

8.1   Prepare a checklist setting out the skills needed by a manager for influencing a section of the Accounts Department to accept a new flexitime arrangement.

8.2   You have been carrying out an investigation as an independent consultant into the payroll administration of a Government Agency working in the field of agriculture. Following your investigation you have a number of proposals to put forward which include:

- computerisation of the payroll systems, which will involve expenditure (hardware, software and training), but also cost savings through time-saving and reduction of errors

- the need to restructure the staffing, which will result in changes in job descriptions and will require staff to be trained in computer skills – but there will be no redundancies

Task

Describe:

(a)   Your plan for approaching the management of the Agency to persuade them to adopt your proposals and the techniques you would use to make them feel comfortable with the proposals.

(b)   Your suggestions to the management of the Agency about how they would sell the idea to the employees in the payroll section, and what techniques they could use to put their point of view across.

K & U : N V Q 9

Techniques for reviewing recommendations through cost-benefit analysis

Pages 66-67 in the text

1   Describe the processes you need to carry out to perform a cost-benefit analysis.

2   Procter Sportswear Ltd is considering a project to improve its credit control system. In order to do this the company will need to employ one extra member of staff at a cost of £16,000 a year. The company will also need to purchase straightaway a new computer system costing £2,000.

   This new member of staff and computer system are expected to speed up cash flow and reduce bad debts, saving the company an estimated £20,000 a year.

   You are to use discounted cash flow to produce a numerical assessment of the costs and benefits of this proposed project over the next five years and to calculate the net present value of the project. The company uses a cost of capital of 10%. The factors to be used are: Year 1 0.909, Year 2 0.826, Year 3 0.751, Year 4 0.683, Year 5 0.621. (Nb this technique was covered in your study of Unit 6).

   On the basis of this calculation briefly evaluate the proposed project from a financial viewpoint.

K & U : Diploma 9, NVQ 10

Principles of supervision and delegation

Pages 70-71 in the text

1   Explain the principles of good supervision – ie what makes a 'good' manager.

2   Tuscany Travel is a company which organises 'activity breaks' – eg cycling, bird watching and cooking holidays – in the Tuscany region of Italy. The owner, Luigi Pirandelli, has recently appointed a new General Manager, Frank Thompson. Frank has carried out a major review of the way in which the business operates and his conclusions are:

   (a)   His deputy managers are lazy. As a result he now calls them in every day to keep an eye on them. His predecessor only saw them every two weeks or so.

   (b)   The departmental sections are not working efficiently, in his opinion. As a result he now visits the sections run by his deputy managers virtually every day.

   Frank has also told his managers not to make any major decisions without asking him first.

   Morale of all the staff at Tuscany Travel has declined and customer service standards have dropped since all this happened and the owner is asking himself if Frank is really up to the job.

   You are to explain what is wrong with Frank Thompson's approach to dealing with these problems and make suggestions for what would be a better, more effective, approach.

K&U: NVQ 11, Diploma 10

Principles of fostering effective working relationships, building teams and motivating staff

Pages 70, 72-73 in the text

1   Describe <u>six</u> ways in which a manager can create an effective team out of the employees working in his or her section.

2   'Motivation is the key'.

   (a)   List six examples of ways in which a manager can motivate employees to work effectively.

   (b)   Give a brief description of an accounting job – any job will do – then assess it against the list of motivation factors provided by Maslow or the list from the 2003 survey (both quoted on page 72). What are the weaknesses of this job in providing motivation? What are its strong points?

K&U: NVQ 12, Diploma 11

How the accounting systems of an organisation are affected by its organisational structure, its Management Information Systems, its administrative systems and procedures and the nature of its business transactions

Pages 53-55 in the text

1   Wayne has just got a job with Sportalive Limited, a chain of six sports equipment shops. He is working in the accounts department of the main shop based in Liverpool. The other five shops are in Birkenhead, St Helens, Maghull, Southport and Formby. The accounting system is largely manual and each branch self-accounting, with its own bank account. Each shop has a point of sale electronic terminal for debit and credit card transactions. It is the job of the accounting staff at the Liverpool store to collate all the accounting information (mostly by email) and to make the major decisions.

(a)   What type of organisational structure will illustrate a business organised in this way?

(b)   What problems might arise for Sportalive Limited in respect of the normal accounting functions of purchasing, stock control, cash and payment handling, management accounts and payroll?

(c)   What solutions could be adopted to solve these problems?

2   What type of accounting system would you expect to find in the following?

(a)   a sole trader electrician

(b)   a local authority

(c)   an online retail business run by a husband and wife partnership, selling garden statues and gnomes

K&U: NVQ 13, Diploma 12

The overview of the organisation's business and its critical external relationships (customers/clients, suppliers, etc)

Pages 51-52 in the text

The 'business' of an organisation – ie what it 'does' – will vary according to its function, whether it is in the private sector or the public sector, or whether it provides a manufactured product or a service. The nature of the 'business' will to some extent determine the 'critical external relationships' with people such as customers or clients and suppliers. This in turn will affect the operation of the accounting system.

1   Describe the 'business' of the BBC and explain who its 'customers' are. How do they pay for the product offered, and how does this impact on the accounting system?

     For further information, visit www.bbc.co.uk

2   Choose a well-known business in the private sector, preferably a public limited company. Describe what its 'business' is, ie its product(s) and who its customers and suppliers are. How does the accounting system of the business deal with the customers and suppliers? For example – is selling and supply on a cash or credit basis? What payment systems are used?

K&U: NVQ 14, Diploma 13

The purpose, structure and organisation of the accounting function and its relationships with other functions within the organisation

Pages 56-57 in the text

1   Draw up an organisation chart of the accounting system of the organisation that you are investigating, either for real, or as part of a Case Study exercise. The chart should include the various accounting areas of activity, eg sales ledger, purchase ledger, payroll. You should make a copy of the chart (ie you should have two copies in total).

On one of the copies insert labelling for each of the areas of activity, explaining the purpose of each area of activity.

2   This can only be answered if you have answered the previous question.

On the second copy of the organisation chart insert labels showing how each of the accounting areas of activity relates to other functional areas within the organisation.

Note: for guidance on how to draw up the charts, see pages 56 and 57.

K&U: NVQ 15, Diploma 14

Who controls the supply of resources (equipment, materials, information and people) within the organisation

Pages 58-59 in the text

1   Describe the various classes of resources mentioned in the K&U item above (ie equipment, materials, information and people) as they relate to the organisation you are investigating or an organisation with which you are familiar. (Note: you do not need to describe financial resources for the purposes of this question).

2   Identify the people who control those resources in the organisation you are investigating or in an organisation with which you are familiar. If you wish you could set out those individuals in the form of an organisation chart illustrating the hierarchy in the organisation.

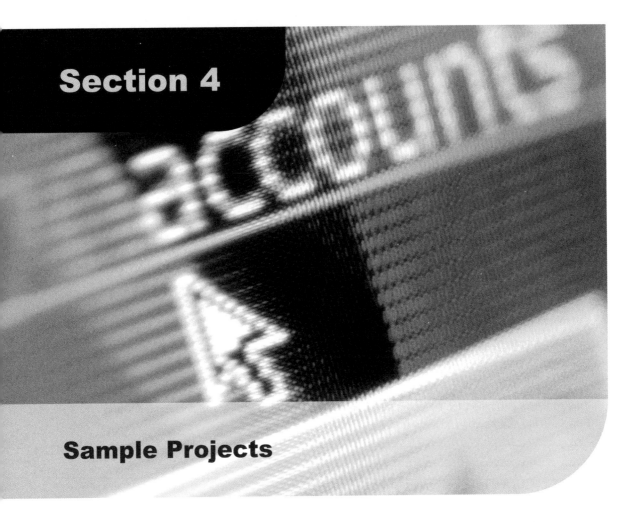

Section 4

Sample Projects

This Section contains sample material adapted and extracted from two original student Projects:

- Heiss Products Limited – a manufacturer of plumbing insulation products

- Easy Freeze Limited – a company specialising in the installation and servicing of refrigeration systems

The aim of this section is to provide guidance to the areas covered in a typical Project. A frequent question asked by students is "How do I get started?" – the problem being a lack of familiarity with what is required. It is hoped that the following pages may help.

These Projects are not claimed to be 'model' reports and you should not necessarily reproduce the layouts shown, but they give a good idea of the issues raised when analysing an accounting system. You should note that:

- Format and style of presentation may vary considerably – remember that there is no 'set' format for a report, the requirement being that all the necessary elements should be present (see page 32 for a recommended list of report sections).

- Appendices have been omitted.

- Names and locations have been changed to preserve confidentiality.

Sample project 1:
Heiss Products Limited

Note that each section of your Project should start on a new page. For the sake of economy of space and consideration for the rainforests this practice has not always been followed in this text.

HEISS LIMITED

THE IMPLEMENTATION OF A BACS PAYMENT SYSTEM TO REDUCE THE AMOUNT OF TIME AND PAPERWORK INVOLVED IN PAYING SUPPLIERS.

Submitted by: A S Tudent

AAT student membership number: N002007

Date: March 20-5

This report is submitted for assessment of competence in Unit 10 'Managing Systems and People in the Accounting Environment'.

LIST OF CONTENTS

Aim

Company Background

The Existing System for Paying Suppliers

Weaknesses of the Existing System

Prevention of Fraud

Improving the System

Making the Decision

Implementing the New System

Conclusion

Appendices

PROJECT AIM

The aim of this project is to identify and implement a system to reduce the amount of time and paperwork involved in paying suppliers whilst maintaining high levels of accuracy, security and fraud control.

COMPANY BACKGROUND

Heiss Products first set out as a distributor of pipe insulation to UK merchants in 1989 and soon expanded to supply to the DIY chains. In 1991 there was an opportunity to purchase a business to manufacture stitched felt that was considered to be lucrative and in line with the products already offered, and so the purchase went ahead. Jon Mattersen (Director) was ambitious to expand the business and increase the product range, so when he was offered to buy a tank and cylinder jacket making business in 1992 there was no hesitation. Throughout the following years the range has increased further in the distribution of water storage cisterns, fibreglass, loft insulation, expanding foam, vermiculite and an innovative plastic plumbing system. (See Appendix 1 for full Product Guide).

The current business is still to supply merchants and DIY chains but we also have a Government contract by the name of "Conserve Energy", this is a scheme whereby people on low income and the elderly can insulate their homes under a grant scheme either fully or partially funded. This scheme requires all the core products; jackets, fibre and insulation. Initially Heiss traded directly with the contractors but soon realised the level of customer service required was different to that demanded by the merchants. At this point the biggest customer was R&S Insulation, which was a newly formed company who had a good reputation and impressive customer service recognised in the market place – but lacked financial stability.

In 1996 the two Companies merged and continue to trade separately. R&S Insulation took over the Government Scheme business whilst Heiss supply all the products. Within twelve months they'd turned the business round and increased the market sector by 50% as the Government was investing money into the scheme and they were able to acquire and retain new business.

At present Heiss is a major manufacturer of tank and cylinder jackets with a significant influence in the market place. To retain this position we offer high quality products and services backed up with a team of friendly and helpful staff. As quoted by one of our major suppliers "Over the course of the last few years Heiss have introduced extended and improved product ranges that are consistently delivered on time. Their staff are knowledgeable and always ring back in response to enquiries. This support is matched by their willingness to "go that extra mile" to help gain new business". This comment is reproduced in the Product Guide in Appendix 1.

The offices of the Company are based just outside of Farmchurch on a Business Park. The company is the sole occupier and has a converted barn as an office block along with two outbuildings. One, a new purpose built factory, houses the manufacturing process of the jackets and the other stores products for distribution. We have two vehicles of our own which are out on a daily basis distributing products; in addition to these we use two local hauliers and a courier company for customers who are located in remote areas.

The accounts department shares office facilities with the Sales team who process orders received direct from customers and via the network of agents across the country. The role of the writer includes all aspects of the sales and purchase ledger along with the production of monthly sales reports and other duties as requested, (see Appendix 3 for full job description). The accounts department aims to be accurate, effective and efficient in meeting and exceeding the expectations of customers, suppliers, agents and internal personnel.

THE EXISTING SYSTEM FOR PAYING SUPPLIERS

The existing system for paying suppliers by cheque is detailed below:-

1   As invoices are received from suppliers they are matched with corresponding delivery notes that in turn have been checked by the purchasing department and have the relevant purchase order attached. Checks are made to ensure the correct amount of product has been received and charged at the order price, if there are any discrepancies then debit notes are raised.

2   Invoices are entered onto the suppliers' ledgers on a daily basis and then filed away awaiting payment.

3   As statements are received at the end of each month these are reconciled to ensure that all invoices relating to each month are entered onto the system. Copies are requested of any missing invoices and these are then processed.

4   Cheques are written prior to dispatch of payment on the 10th, 15th, 21st and last day of each month.

5   Cheques are written based on the amount showing outstanding on the ledger for each supplier, in line with their settlement terms. The system has a facility to input settlement dates on the profile of each account and from this creditor reports are produced detailing which suppliers are to be paid on which day of the month.

6   Once the cheques have been written they are attached to the invoices so that the Director signing them is able to spot check invoices, a method of fraud prevention.

7   The next step is to pay the invoices off on the system and produce remittance advices for ease of payment allocation at the suppliers.

8   Payment on the system involves accessing each account and making a payment, this requires the following information to be entered to complete the transaction; date, cheque number and amount. Once this information has been entered the payment is matched to the relevant invoices to clear them off the system and produce the remittance advice.

9   The remittance advices are printed and attached to the cheques and invoices then passed to the Director for signing, the remittance also enables him to see when payment is due so that the cheques can be posted in time to meet the specified settlement dates.

10   Once authorisation has been obtained the cheques are sent via post to suppliers, and the invoices are stamped as paid and filed away.

WEAKNESSES OF THE EXISTING SYSTEM

- Time consuming both for the production and authorisation of each cheque.

- The system is open to fraud as the person producing the cheques could be paying non-genuine invoices that would not always be identified by the Director's spot checks.

- Reliant on the Royal Mail to deliver post on time ensuring settlement dates are adhered to.

- Need to identify and check un-presented cheques to see if they have been lost and if so possibly incurring cancellation bank charges or disallowed settlement discounts. Bank charges are high due to the number of transactions made by cheque.

- Requires postage and stationery increasing costs to the business.

- Reliant on the efficiency of Suppliers' accounting procedures, with reference to receiving payments in time for settlement discounts.

- Signatures could be forged, the Director doesn't see the Bank Reconciliation and therefore would not recognise fraudulent items immediately.

- The Bank Reconciliation has a high number of transactions to reconcile.

- If a cheque number is incorrectly entered on the payment screen it causes difficulty in when reconciling takes place.

- If the Director omits to sign one cheque in a batch and is then out of the office for a period of time it can cause problems in payments being overdue.

- Sometimes payment runs are prepared a week or more in advance if the Director is scheduled to be out of the office. As some suppliers require payment within seven days to be eligible for settlement discounts, it is possible for a deadline of this type to be missed or paid outside the normal terms.

PREVENTION OF FRAUD

Throughout the purchasing function there are several systems in place to prevent fraud occurring, these are monitored by all levels of the team as specified below:

- When invoices are received they are matched to an official order. The goods on the order are booked onto the system by the purchasing department when they receive the delivery note from the goods inwards section. Goods inwards have a copy of each purchase order raised in order to check the goods received are correctly specified and in the correct quantity.

- Any invoices received that do not quote an order number must be annotated and authorised, by the appropriate department manager.

- Once invoices are passed, either by a corresponding purchase order or authorised by management, the accounts assistant enters them on the purchase ledger.

- At month end all supplier balances are reconciled to statements so any invoice entered onto the cash account, a common area of fraud, is checked with the supplier as being outstanding. The cash account is used for one off purchases only.

- When payments are made to suppliers the Managing Director authorises the payments using the original invoices to which the payment relates in order to spot check any transaction he so wishes. Being a "hands on" Director he is able to identify any suspect products from sources he is unaware of.

- The Accountant who again has a "hands on" role transmits the payment runs. With the company being fairly small she is familiar with the suppliers and goods purchased from each one.

- The completed payment runs and remittances are passed back to the purchase ledger clerk to send to suppliers providing an opportunity to confirm that the Accountant has not added any further transactions after the Director has authorised them.

So, in total, each person dealing with the purchase and payment of goods is checked by at least two others and any queries resolved immediately.

IMPROVING THE SYSTEM

It was identified that there were two available options for improving the system.

1. Printing cheques

2. BACS systems

Once the alternatives were identified they needed to be investigated in more detail taking into consideration how they would improve the system.

1. **Printing cheques.**

   Pros

   This would shorten the amount of time taken to write the cheques as the system would automatically print the inputted dates onto each cheque, allocate it a cheque number and print the suppliers name and amount.

   Cheques returned to drawer due to erroneous completion will be minimised.

   Cons

   Fraud would still be possible if the spot checks of the Director did not identify non-genuine invoices.

   The Director still needs to sign each cheque so his role would remain unchanged in this process.

   A significant amount of funds may be sitting in a current account awaiting clearance of a cheque when this could be invested for several days.

   Printed stationery would also need to be purchased at an additional cost. Currently remittances are printed on plain listing paper costing in the region of £15.00 for 2,000 sheets, printed cheques attached to remittances would carry an artwork charge of approximately £70.00 and then £55.00 per 1,000 sheets. Also this limits the Company to one supplier.

   The reliance is still on the Royal Mail to deliver in time for settlements.

2. **BACS Systems**

   Pros

   A BACS system gives more control over the dates payments are received by suppliers.

   It would involve a list, (detailing supplier name, ID code and amount payable) of up to 35 transactions at any one time requiring only one signature.

   Bank reconciliations at month end would be easier as there would not be so many transactions throughout the month, each list of 35 transactions amounts to one bank statement entry for the total amount.

   Cash flow would be easier to control to maximise investment, as clearance of payments will be more predictable.

No need for the purchase of specialised stationery, as remittances would be printed onto plain A4 paper thus reducing costs: the approximate cost of 500 sheets of plain A4 paper is £2.50.

Remittance advices could be faxed or emailed thus reducing postage costs.

Cons

Fraud may still be possible as once a BACS listing has been prepared and authorised, further transactions could be added.

Suppliers' details could be changed to a fraudulent bank account.

There are two types of BACS system available, one linked to the current system and the other, although not linked to the current system, is on a separate system that is linked directly to the bank.

MAKING THE DECISION

It was decided to introduce a BACS system as this was seen as a way forward offering the control and flexibility that is now a necessity.

The two BACS systems were investigated:-

1.   **The Linked System**

      Pros

      This is a free upgrade to our in house Pegasus Opera accounting package.

      The system involves a password login and features can be restricted; for example, all users could produce the BACS listing while only managers could transmit.

      Remittances can be faxed or emailed direct without printing provided all the required information is detailed on the customer profile.

      Cons

      There is an annual charge for the provision of a help desk at £480 + VAT.

      All supplier bank details are stored within the system. If there is a system failure, this may cause problems. Also fraud is a problem as bank details could be changed by the purchase ledger clerk.

2.   **The Non-Linked system**

      Pros

      This is a separate system with a direct link to the bank enabling ease of access to the Company's banking details.

      This is a password-protected system.

      This system will be charged at £20.00 per quarter and 24p per transaction. We pay approximately 100 suppliers per month (a full listing of suppliers is seen in Appendix 7 although only the highlighted accounts are currently live and not each of these is used every month), therefore our annual costs will be in the region of £368 + VAT, compared to the help desk charge, shown above, alone illustrates a saving in admin costs.

      Suppliers' bank details are stored and given a short code, the facility to amend bank details requires a high level password.

      The bank provides a free help desk.

      Cons

      A new PC will be required to install this program.

      After further investigation and discussion, the decision was made to introduce the non-linked system. Although initially the linked system was a free upgrade, the long term costs would be considerably more. Despite the costs involved, the main reasons for choosing the non-linked system are the security features and the ease of use. Also, this system allows the Accountant access to view our bank accounts and transactions on a daily basis to identify incoming payments from our customers, giving greater control over the day to day cash flow.

We felt that the linked system could be potentially open to fraud; once the payment listing had been printed and authorised further transactions could be added prior to the Accountant transmitting the file without their knowledge, as the transfer is completed by electronically transferring a file of payments to the bank which clear on a specified date. Remittances would not be printed, as these would be faxed straight from the system after payments had been allocated and transmitted. These transactions would remain undetected until appearing on a statement during the bank reconciliation process at month end. A purchase ledger clerk who allocates payments completes this, and so this was perceived as a weakness in the fraud prevention methods.

IMPLEMENTING THE NEW SYSTEM

- The bank installed the programme onto an existing unused PC within the Company, so there was no need to purchase a new one. The bank also provided a day's training. The system is self-explanatory and easy to use, with the added confidence that a free help desk is just a telephone call away.

- Prior to implementing the system, we needed to obtain information from our suppliers of their bank details (see Appendix 4) and input them into the system, which then allocates them a unique identification code with one, two or three digits for future use (see Appendix 5). The inputting took almost a day, but now each supplier has his or her own ID code, which is all that is required when entering a transaction other than the amount of the payment. Additional suppliers can be added at any point in time.

- The Purchase Ledger Clerk produces the BACS listing, (see Appendix 6), totals it and then the Accountant inputs each line ensuring the ID code is correct and that the total can be confirmed, as the Bank PC gives a total of the transactions entered prior to transmission. To reduce the risk of fraud the Purchase Ledger Clerk produces the listing, totals it and signs it before it is passed to the Director for authorising. The Accountant then processes the list on the bank link and can easily identify and eliminate any transactions that have been added after the authorisation process.

- As this was a whole new concept, it was decided to implement the new system on a three month trial to pay our Agents their monthly commission. We felt that this way we would get feedback, both positive and negative. We wanted to be sure that the system performed to our expectations prior to introducing it across the board.

- The system has a deadline of 4pm for transactions to be processed, in order for it to clear the funds the next day to appear in the destination account on the morning of the third day, (day one being the processing day). Upon successful completion of the trial we started processing the payments at 3.30pm to ensure that the 4pm deadline was met to allow sufficient time for any last minute payments that we might need to make. The system also allows the transaction date to be set in the future which will ensure payments can still run smoothly whilst members of staff are on holiday or out of the office. We tested this function on the third month after successfully transmitting the previous payments.

CONCLUSION

- The objective has been achieved, a new system has been identified and implemented that reduces the amount of time in paying suppliers' whilst maintaining high levels of accuracy, security and fraud control.

- The chosen system is a BACS system linked directly to the bank that transmits payments to suppliers' bank accounts and allows access to our bank accounts on a daily basis, showing up to date balances and transactions. The number of transactions through our account has been considerably reduced resulting in time saved during the bank reconciliation process at month end. Costs have been reduced as each transaction now costs only 24p as opposed to 56p previously, remittances are printed on A4 paper costing approximately 50p per month (£2.50 per 500 sheets) when previously printed on listing paper costing 75p per month (£15.00 per 2000 sheets) and faxed so reducing postage costs of 27p per item to a faxed cost of 5p. These add up to a total saving of £54.25 per month based on 100 transactions.

- We still have a chequebook facility for suppliers dealt with on a one-off basis, as it is not worth setting up an account on the system or obtaining the required bank details if they will never be used again.

- The system allows much more flexibility within the accounts department as payment runs can be set up to be transmitted during staff holidays, so there is no longer any need to prepare payment runs weeks in advance as three days is sufficient for the processing. The remittances are faxed so there is not the two day postal delay.

- As outlined in the "prevention of fraud" we have identified and upgraded our processes within the scope of the new system and are constantly reviewing any areas where improvements can be made.

Appendices

1. Group Product Guide

2. Organisation Chart

3. Job Description

4. Request for Bank Details

5. Customer Account List

6. BACS Payment Form

7. Supplier Listing

Sample project 2:
Easy Freeze Limited

EASY FREEZE LIMITED

AN ANALYSIS OF THE JOB COSTING SYSTEM AND THE IMPLEMENTATION OF A SAGE JOB COSTING COMPUTER SYSTEM

Submitted by: A N Otherstudent

AAT student membership number: N002008

Date: March 20-5

This report is submitted for assessment of competence in Unit 10 'Managing Systems and People in the Accounting Environment'.

LIST OF CONTENTS

Organisation Background

Analysis of The Present System

Findings

Recommendations

Implementation of the New System

Benefits of the New System

Assessment of the New System

Actions Taken in Response

Conclusion

Appendices

ORGANISATION BACKGROUND

- Easy Freeze Limited (EFL) is active throughout the UK, specialising in the installation and servicing of refrigeration equipment.

- Easy Freeze Limited was formed on 1st November 1976. The original company was formed by John Milton and Sid Furlong and started working mainly in used commercial refrigeration equipment.

- In 1979 EFL started working with Carpigiani of Bologna, Italy, promoting soft ice-cream machines, slush machines and cream whipping machines. In 1985 "Giovanni's" was opened in Budborough as part of a marketing and promotion campaign to market specialist equipment in the development of the Italian Ice Cream Parlour.

- In 1996 the Company took over Shaston Refrigeration customers due to retirement of the director and were made exclusive agents for the UK by Bocchini. They also started to work with Star SRL importing furniture for Bars, Cafes and Ice Cream Parlours as well as promoting and installing Air Conditioning Systems.

- EFL operates from a new modern office suite in Budborough, where they have a meeting room complete with many material samples for its shopfitting requirements. They also offer a CAD design service with staff fully trained in design and construction of counter systems. There is a showroom downstairs promoting the various refrigeration equipment on offer as well as various other catering requirements. Tom, Sid Furlong's son helps with the design office and also offers ice-cream demonstrations to potential customers.

- The company also has its own Service Department with fully trained engineers. They carry out installations as well as repairs and servicing. EFL also has a team of shop fitters who specialise in installing wooden counters and laminate flooring and panelling. They work on a sub-contract basis.

- Last year, it was decided to separate the company into Sales and Service divisions to give a more accurate overview for the accounts department. The Sales Department is run by Sid Furlong, assisted in administration by Sarah Foot and a team of sales people. He is also in charge of the running of the design office and promotions.

- The service side is run by John Milton, assisted by Kulvinder Singh who is also the Office Manager and is in charge of organising the day to day jobs for the engineers. John Milton is in charge of quoting for service installations including air conditioning and cellar cooling systems.

- Anne Jones joined the company in 1999 on a self employed basis providing support to Kulvinder Singh and Kurt Schmidt, the company accountant. Her main duties were to enter the service calls on Microsoft Outlook, enter purchase and sales invoices, enter payments and update a manual job costing system. It was the job costing system that was proving to be inadequate and it became her job to improve and update the system to enable management to obtain important and accurate information.

See APPENDIX 1: COMPANY ORGANISATION CHART

ANALYSIS OF THE PRESENT SYSTEM

The present system for costing jobs is performed on a spreadsheet using Microsoft Excel. When a quote is accepted by the customer, an order is placed. This order is entered on Microsoft Outlook and a new client account is set up on the Sage Accounts package. Subsequently a new account is also set up in Microsoft Excel using the current job costing format and that job is given a job costing number. Presently there are three categories for job costings: Bocchini Installations, Exhibitions and 'other' installations.

See APPENDIX 2: CURRENT JOB COSTING FORMAT – EXCEL

As can been seen from the present format, there are various columns where information has to be entered regarding costs directly incurred by that job. These include engineers worksheets, capital items purchased, consumables purchased, freight charges and van hire as well as fuel and commission. The job number would be written on each worksheet or invoice and entered in the appropriate column.

FINDINGS

- Over a period of time, it was apparent that this system had various inadequacies. The main problem was that worksheets were being overlooked, especially if the engineers did not put the job number on them. Also purchase invoices were having to be entered twice, once on Sage and once for the job costing package. As these were passing through different people and departments, the job numbers were also sometimes not put on them and so some purchases, especially consumables were being overlooked.

- There was also the problem of column space. As the job progressed, more columns would sometimes have to be added for other expenses such as bank charges, food and accommodation for engineers and sub contract labour. This meant that the reports would run over two pages and would have to be stuck together to make sense of the figures. This not only looked unprofessional, but made reading the reports awkward. Also, if the formulas were not set up properly, the columns would not add up correctly. These would all then have to be checked manually and amended, taking more valuable time.

- There was also the issue regarding Downtime. This is time spent by the engineers and surveyor of the job which cannot be charged to the customer. The company needed to know the amount of Downtime each month in order to make adequate allowances within the costing structure and also to ascertain whether the engineers were performing to standard. At the same time, the company had expanded to take on more suppliers and different types of installations such as furniture and fittings and Orion Installations. These were now growing and needed to be categorised properly. All the above issues needed to be improved and a new system would have to be found that could incorporate all the fundamental characteristics required for accurate job costing and would be able to produce accurate and varied reports covering all criteria.

RECOMMENDATIONS

It was evident from the problems described above, that an improved system was needed. The new system would have to adhere to the following strategy:

1   Tighter control over engineer's timesheets. A check would have to be put in place to ensure that the engineers put the correct job number on their timesheets.

2   Purchase invoices to be passed through one central control (office manager) to be coded for accounts purposes and the correct job number.

3   Procedures put in place for control over stock items used against the various job numbers.

4   New job costing package to be purchased to cut down on time spent entering information and double checking figures.

5   Ideally, the new system would be integrated in some way with the accounts package to cut down on duplication of entries.

6   New job costing package required to print detailed, accurate and up-to-the-minute reports which are well laid out and easy to understand, for use in management decisions.

7   New job costing package required that can incorporate an accurate Downtime feature which would give detailed reports on each engineer's Downtime and highlight problem areas.

8   One person to be put in charge of entering the information for the job costing procedure and made responsible for making sure all relevant information is given to them by appointed persons. This person would also be responsible for collating and filing the information for each job number and printing out reports for management when a job was finished.

IMPLEMENTATION OF CHANGE

- The first thing that was decided was that Kulvinder Singh, the office manager, who was also in charge of the service side of the business, would oversee the project. She had always been aware of the inadequacies of the present system. Anne Jones was to be put in charge of the day to day running of the job costing procedure. As she had experienced the old system and was familiar with the problems being caused, she was the ideal candidate to help find a better system and was prepared to undertake the training for a new computer program. It was also decided that Sarah Foot, who runs the Sales Administration would take an active part in controlling the new system.

- After much deliberation and searching through various relevant information, EFL decided to purchase the Sage Job Costing Package. This was chosen mainly because it is fully integrated with the Sage Accounts and Payroll packages already being used by EFL and because there was a local company who supplied the software and support for the system as well as in house training for the staff. Although it cost around £300 for the package with training costs on top, it was deemed as worthwhile investment as it would be saving time and providing the necessary information required for accurate costing.

SAGE JOB COSTING PACKAGE

Sage Job Costing was chosen because it is designed to integrate with Sage Line 50 Accounts package and Sage Payroll to provide a comprehensive cost management system. These are the accounts and payroll packages already being used by EFL. Sage Job Costing shares common information with Sage Line 50 ledgers which means you only need to enter information in one place for it to be available to both programs. The ledgers which are linked as follows:

Purchases

When you enter purchase invoices or credit notes, you can use the suppliers set up in Sage Line 50. If it is a new supplier, the information can be entered in the Sage Job Costing package and it will appear in the accounts. When you post the purchase invoices and credit notes, it automatically updates the relevant suppliers purchase history in the accounts package.

Sales

When you create a new job, you can attach an existing customer to a job. If the job is for a new customer, you can create a new customer in the job costing package and it will show up in the accounts package.

Invoicing

If you want to bill customers, Sage Job Costing can create sales invoices which can be transferred to the Sage Line 50 invoicing ledger. You can then update the service invoice in Sage Line 50, which will update the customer's sales history.

Nominal

When you post purchase or banking transactions you need to enter an existing Sage Line 50 nominal ledger code. When the transactions are posted they will automatically update the nominal ledger history.

Stock

Stock transactions automatically decrease or increase stock levels and update the stock history in Sage Line 50. In Sage Job Costing you can choose whether or not stock transactions affect stock profitability in Sage Line 50.

Bank

You can post bank, credit card and cash payments to the relevant accounts in Sage Line 50.

BENEFITS OF THE NEW SYSTEM

As can be seen from the Life Cycle in Appendix 3, the Sage Job Costing package follows the job through from beginning to end incorporating all aspects of expenditure. Job costing can now take on a whole new meaning than just a few figures on a spreadsheet. The costings can now be broken down into great detail which will help personnel understand the precise breakdown of a job. This will ensure that jobs are managed more efficiently in future. This will also be beneficial in helping to prepare estimates for future work more quickly and accurately.

See APPENDIX 3: A JOB LIFE CYCLE WITHIN SAGE JOB COSTING

Having an integrated system will also reduce administration and production costs. Productivity should be increased as the program will help decide the best use of personnel, materials and machines. Detailed monitoring of costs and revenues will help optimise cashflow for the business.

Over a period of time, it will also be possible to determine which type of jobs are the most profitable – this will play a large part in making decisions over sales and service installations. As the company had decided to split the Sales and Service expenditure and revenue, the new system would help them to make important management decisions as to the profitability of certain installations. As reports can be looked at at any time, it is possible to keep a close eye on expenditure and cut down on losses on certain jobs. In this way, jobs can be monitored through the whole cycle and costs can be cut to ensure all expenditure is incorporated into the selling price and a profit is attained. The system can also be monitored and handled by one designated person.

See APPENDIX 4: COMPLETED JOB COSTING REPORT AND PROFITABILITY REPORT.

ASSESSMENT OF THE NEW SYSTEM

When the system was installed, Office Support came to train Anne Jones, Kulvinder Singh and Sarah Foot. Although Anne Jones was to be put in charge of the day to day running of the package, it was Kulvinder Singh and Sarah Foot's responsibility to make sure all relevant information was passed to her. Engineers time sheets would be checked and signed off by Kulvinder Singh as well as Service Purchase Invoices. These would be married off with relevant delivery notes and purchase orders, the nominal code would be written on the invoices as well as the relevant job number. The same would be done by Sarah Foot for the Sales division Purchase Invoices and timesheets for Sales engineers.

See APPENDIX 5: TIMESHEET AND PURCHASE INVOICE

As can be seen from the timesheets in Appendix 4, it was sometimes very confusing to decipher what exactly the engineers had been doing and which job it would be billed to. Sometimes, they would be working on two or three jobs in the workshop and the time would need to be allocated to the various jobs. Also, there was confusion as to what cost categories the actual engineers tasks were to be put against. This resulted in Anne Jones spending a great deal of her time trying to find out exactly what was to be entered against each time sheet.

Another problem that arose was the allocation of job numbers. As Anne Jones was only in 1 or 2 days a week, job numbers needed to be allocated to new jobs coming in during the rest of the week. This meant that they would have to wait until Anne Jones came in the following week before any costs could be allocated to the job. Problems occurred when both the Sales and Service departments would use the next available job number and not liaise with each other. This resulted in the same job number being allocated to two different jobs, causing great confusion and jeopardising the whole system.

On top of this the Sales department could not agree as to the definition of Downtime and there were discrepancies in entries. Finally, the most crucial problem that came to light was that there was no procedure in place which alerted anyone as to when a job was complete and costings could be run with the knowledge that all costs had been entered. It is quite common in large installations that there are problems with the final snagging jobs and these can run on well after the main installation has been completed. This does however mean that the fitters final invoice and any subsequent invoices for extra materials used will not have been received into the accounts department.

Appendix 6 sets out a memo which was sent by Kulvinder Singh, Office Manager, to all staff concerning the problems experienced with job costing.

See APPENDIX 6: MEMO – JOB COSTING DATA ENTRY

ACTIONS TAKEN IN RESPONSE TO PROBLEMS WITH NEW SYSTEM

As a result of the memo in Appendix 6, a Management Meeting was held which all staff associated with job costing had to attend. All the problems were addressed and the following recommendations were made and implemented with immediate effect.

duplicated job numbers

A system was set up in Microsoft Word whereby Anne Jones would list all the job numbers and which jobs they represented. The next number was made available to all staff on the network system. This meant that when a new job came in, either Kulvinder Singh or Sarah Foot could access the list on their computers and enter the new job against the subsequent next available job number. They would then fill in a Job Costing sheet detailing the Customer name and address, contact details, job classification, special cost centres and price quoted. The new job number would be listed on the bottom and the sheet put in Anne Jones' tray ready for entry on the Sage job costing package. This meant that no job number would be used twice and jobs could be allocated a job number without having to wait for Anne Jones to come in and allocate one.

see APPENDIX 7: NEW JOB NUMBERS ISSUED/JOB COSTING SHEET

timesheet entries

Instead of Anne Jones having to work off the timesheets, a system was devised and a form designed whereby all the engineers time sheets and any sheets with items taken from stock and used against a job number, were collated by the personnel who were in charge of passing the timesheets and purchase invoices to Anne Jones, ie Kulvinder Singh and Sarah Foot. A wallet file was opened for each job number and all relevant paperwork pertaining to that job was collected in that wallet with Kulvinder keeping all the Service Installation folders in her office and Sarah keeping all the Sales Installation folders. When they were certain a job was near completion and all engineers timesheets and purchase invoices had been collected, they filled in a total job sheet as can be seen in Appendix 7. In this way, they would cut down dramatically on Anne Jones's time and all paperwork was in one place for each job, making it easier and quicker to track any discrepancies.

see APPENDIX 8: TOTAL CALCULATION OF JOB COSTING

cost categories

Anne Jones printed off a Master Cost List, which listed all the categories for the various tasks undertaken by the engineers and this was given to Sarah Foot and Kulvinder Singh to be able to put the tasks described on the timesheets into the correct categories for entry on the computer, therefore eliminating any doubt as to what category to use.

see APPENDIX 9: MASTER COST CODE LIST

downtime

It was decided that any time spent on a job by an engineer that was not or could not be charged for would be classed as Downtime.

SEE APPENDIX 10: DOWNTIME REPORT

job progress reports

Jim Mallett, the Project Coordinator, was the only person in the company who would always be aware of any snagging problems with all live jobs. A procedure was put in place whereby Jim Mallett would present Anne Jones with a monthly report on all the current installations. This means that Anne Jones has a regular update as to which jobs can be finalised and reports printed off for management.

see APPENDIX 11: MONTHLY REPORT ON ALL INSTALLATIONS

CONCLUSION

- Having now run the system for three months with the improvements in place, it has been possible for the company to have a complete picture of the precise costing for each job that can be relied upon to be correct. It has virtually eradicated the possibility of engineers fraudulently claiming overtime on installations.

  Since running the system, it has highlighted the large amount of time spent on Downtime by the engineers.

  SEE APPENDIX 11: DOWNTIME COSTINGS CHART FOR THE LAST 6.5 MONTHS

- This has resulted in a change in how the engineers time is used and redundancies were made to cut unnecessary costs. A large saving in wasted time and expense has been made as a result of this report.

- Using the Sage Job Costing package correctly has also resulted in management being able to identify products and services which are costing more than originally budgeted for. This has resulted in EFL looking for new suppliers and negotiating with current suppliers for better discounts and services.

- Changing the previous Job Costing system to Sage Job Costing has benefited the Company greatly in giving Management more control over expenditure as well as optimising the cashflow for the business by detailed monitoring of costs and revenue.

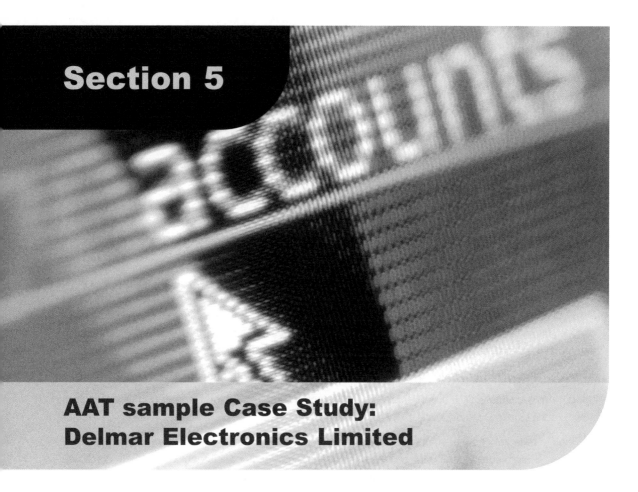

Section 5

AAT sample Case Study: Delmar Electronics Limited

This Section contains sample material issued by AAT in 2003 when the current Unit 10 was introduced, and is reproduced with their kind permission. The aim of the material is to provide guidance for AAT Unit 10 Simulations. It is not to be used as a live Simulation. The material (which is AAT copyright) contains:

- ▪ **Case Study**

  A profile of Delmar Electronics Limited, which manufactures a specialist range of semi-conductor test equipment. The profile includes:
  - details of accounting personnel
  - a description of the accounting system
  - a narrative of recent events to set the scene
  - recent accounts

- ▪ **Candidate briefing**

  Instructions to candidates about the writing of the report, including the need to cover Knowledge & Understanding and Performance Criteria.

- ▪ **Notes for Assessors**

- ▪ **Suggested Report Extracts**

HEALTH WARNING! The contents of this sample material may seem complex and, at times, daunting. The assessment requirements will, however, allow for a simpler treatment.

Project Case Study: Delmar Electronics Limited

THE COMPANY'S BACKGROUND AND MANAGEMENT

It is now April 2003. Your name is Tony Bush, and you are employed as an accounting systems technician with Delmar Electronics Limited (DEL).

The company was established six years ago by three colleagues, Richard West, Omar Sangha and John Bryce, who all knew each other well from working together in the electronics sector. Richard and Omar were both working at the time for Fort Technology Plc, a large quoted manufacturer of semi-conductor testing equipment. Richard was the technical director and Omar a technical sales manager. John Bryce was employed as production manager in a similar electronics manufacturing company.

Four years ago Elaine Candler joined DEL as finance director, the fourth member of the board.

Their current positions in DEL are: Richard West (Managing Director), Elaine Candler (Finance Director), Omar Sangha (Sales Director), John Bryce (Production Director).

From their knowledge of the electronics business the company's founders believed there was a hole in the market for a high quality specialist range of semi-conductor test equipment. Using their combined expertise they were able to produce a convincing business plan. This enabled them from the outset to raise sufficient capital to launch DEL as a significant player in this particular sector.

Six years later the company has grown rapidly to a turnover of over £20 million, with net assets of over £3 million and with a workforce of over 200 employees. Details for DEL's accounts for the year to 31 March 2002 are given in Appendix 1.

ACCOUNTING AND OTHER INFORMATION TECHNOLOGY SYSTEMS

Most of the company's information systems have been in place for between 4 - 6 years and are in need of updating.

At present the principal systems are as follows:

- The main financial accounting system, including integrated general, purchase and sales ledgers. This operates in MSDOS and holds data in a non-relational database.
- A stand-alone full absorption costing system running on proprietary Wise software.
- A new integrated payroll and personnel database management system running in Windows 98, which was installed 3 months ago.
- A computer aided design/computer aided management (CAD/CAM) system, which is used for the design and control of the production of DEL products.

ACCOUNTING PERSONNEL

ELAINE CANDLER, BA, FCMA, FINANCE DIRECTOR

Elaine, aged 49, has overall responsibility for all accounting, finance, legal and IT issues. Elaine's primary responsibility is to manage the overall financial strategy of the business. Ensuring that capital investments are thoroughly appraised and in line with corporate strategy, that working capital levels are kept to a minimum, that the optimal mix of debt and equity funds DEL, and that its credit rating is maximised. In addition Elaine personally produces the annual company report, including its statutory accounts; deals with all banking and finance issues and fulfils the role of company secretary and handles all legal issues.

WILLIAM WHITELOW, AAT, COMPANY ACCOUNTANT

William, aged 59, has full day-by-day responsibility for the running of the DEL accounts department. He has been employed as company accountant since DEL was founded, and is AAT qualified. Originally William reported directly to the managing director, but since Elaine's appointment as finance director he has reported to her. William supervises the work of the accounting technicians and clerks running the transaction accounting systems, i.e. the general ledger, purchase ledger, and sales ledger, together with the costing system and the payroll and personnel database management system. In addition, William personally produces the monthly management accounts, and approves all payments to suppliers.

The other five Accounts Department staff, which all report to William Whitelow, are:

SHARON EVANS, GENERAL LEDGER CLERK

Sharon, aged 26, is responsible for all data directly requiring input into the general ledger and for producing the end of month trial balance. She is also responsible for maintaining the company's cash book and its petty cash. Sharon has been in the job since she joined DEL three years ago, and has no accounting qualifications. Previously Sharon worked as a trainee personnel officer, but had to change job when her family moved area.

SUE MORAN, PURCHASE LEDGER CLERK

Sue, aged 36, is responsible for all data input into the purchase ledger, and for paying suppliers. Sue, who is William Whitelow's daughter, has been in this job for the past three years, and has foundation level AAT qualifications. Before working on the purchase ledger Sue spent the previous 18 months as the sales ledger clerk.

MOHAMED SINGH, SALES LEDGER CLERK AND CREDIT CONTROLLER

Mohamed, aged 27, is responsible for all data input into the sales ledger, and for the company's credit control. Mohamed has been in the job for the past three years since joining DEL, from Withern Electronics Ltd, where he was the purchase ledger clerk. Mohamed currently has no accounting or credit control qualifications, but has expressed an interest in acquiring some.

DAVID BROWNE, COSTING TECHNICIAN

David, aged 47, is responsible for costing DEL's products. He has been in this job since the company was formed, and his only other previous employer was a furniture manufacturer, where he worked after leaving school until the firm closed just over six years ago. His final position there was as credit controller. David has no accounting qualifications, and has on several occasions expressed his reluctance to undertake any form of personal development or training.

RACHEL FREY, PAYROLL & PERSONNEL DATABASE CLERK

Rachel, aged 22, is responsible for running the monthly payroll (for salaried staff) and weekly payroll (for hourly paid staff), and issuing P45's, P60's and so on. She is also responsible for maintaining the personnel database. Rachel was recruited to do this job two months ago, when the previous clerk left. Rachel has no accounting qualifications, and joined the company straight from university, where she obtained a pass degree in history. The software company who sold DEL the system gave Rachel three day's intensive training on the new payroll and personnel system.

The final member of the accounts team is you, **TONY BUSH, ACCOUNTING SYSTEMS TECHNICIAN.**

You report directly to Elaine Candler. You are aged 26, and are employed largely on reviewing accounting systems, plus any other project work that the finance director or company accountant may ask you to undertake. You have worked for DEL for the past two years and are hoping to complete your AAT qualifications this year. You have experience of working on both sales and general ledgers, but not at DEL.

BUSINESS & ACCOUNTING PRACTICES AND POLICIES

PURCHASES AND SUPPLIER PAYMENTS

The company buyer, George Stewart, is responsible for identifying and liaising with suppliers, and negotiating all contracts and prices with them. George has been in this position for the past four years.

The previous buyer had always followed a policy, set by the DEL board, of dealing with around 150 suppliers and playing one off against another in order to buy any materials or capital items at the lowest possible price available for that individual transaction. Three years ago, however, both George and William Whitelow had attended a seminar on "partnership sourcing", and had recommended to the board that a new policy of dealing with a much smaller number of suppliers on long term contracts should be adopted. The board approved this change and DEL now operates with only around 30 regular suppliers, who are on two to three year contracts with annual price negotiations. The advantage of this policy to DEL is that it can get to know and understand 30 suppliers far better than it can 150, and can get the advantages of long term stability in terms of product quality and prices.

Virtually all purchases are on 30 – 60 day credit terms. The purchase ledger clerk, Sue Moran, checks any new suppliers for financial stability.

All supplier invoices and goods received notes are sent initially to George Stewart, who is responsible for checking that the correct quantities have been received as ordered, and that the invoiced prices are correct. George then passes the approved invoices to Sue Moran who enters them into the purchases ledger, and at the same time makes the appropriate general ledger postings. Every month the purchase ledger system produces an aged creditors listing which identifies those suppliers now due for payment. The company accountant, William Whitelow, is responsible for approving the actual payments to be made, but bearing in mind the company's cash position at the time. Suppliers are, in fact, nearly always paid on time.

Finally, the computer system produces the actual cheques, which are then signed both by William Whitelow and by one of the four directors. Usually this will be Elaine Candler, but when she is away on business, which is quite often the case, Richard West generally countersigns them. Increasingly suppliers are paid by BACS, in which case the BACS payment authority is approved by William and then countersigned by one of the other directors. Neither the sales nor production directors is ever happy about countersigning all the individual cheques, because of the time involved, but are quite happy to put the one countersignature on the BACS payment authority form.

All company cheques are required to have two signatures, the authorised signatories being the four directors and the company accountant.

SALES AND CUSTOMER RECEIPTS

The company's sales force, led by Omar Sangha, is responsible for all dealings with existing customers and for identifying potential new ones. When a new customer is found, the company's policy is generally to trade with them on cash with an order basis of a three month trial period. The sales ledger clerk, Mohamed Singh, is responsible for credit checking these new customers, together with the relevant sales representative. This is to recommend a credit limit, which will apply after the three month trial period. All new credit limits and changes to existing limits are approved by the finance director, or in her absence by the managing director.

DEL has around 250 regular customers – 40 of whom account for 80% of the company's turnover.

The sales ledger clerk, Mohamed Singh, uses the goods dispatched listings as the trigger to produce sales invoices, which in accordance with Elaine Candler's instructions are sent out on a daily basis. All cheque payments received are sent to Mohamed who banks them also on a daily basis. Mohamed is responsible for all the postings to the sales ledger, and for the associated entries in the general ledger.

Sharon Evans produces a monthly bank reconciliation statement, which amongst other things reconciles the cash book to the bank statement and the paying in book to the statement. The reconciliation is then checked by William Whitelow, who formally signs it off as being correct.

Mohamed produces a monthly aged debtors listing and all outstanding debtors more than one month overdue are reviewed with William Whitelow.

All outstanding debtors, more than three months overdue are reviewed both by Elaine Candler and by Omar Sangha.

PAYROLL AND PERSONNEL RECORDS

The company operates with two separate payrolls. Rachel Frey, the payroll and personnel database clerk runs the first every week to pay the hourly paid, largely the shop floor workers. Around 20% of these hourly paid employees are paid in cash, with the rest having payments made directly into their bank accounts via BACS. Those paid in cash collect their pay packets from Rachel's office every Friday, and those paid via BACS have their pay credited to their accounts on the same day. The second payroll is run three days before the last working day of each month to pay the monthly paid staff, which is either management, sales or office staff. All monthly paid employees are paid via BACS.

Once the two payrolls for the month have been finalised William Whitelow draws up a manual cheque payable to the Inland Revenue in respect of income tax and NIC payments. William and one of the four directors sign this cheque.

As well as running the payroll, Rachel also maintains all the personnel records on the same integrated payroll and personnel database management system. This is DEL's newest system, having only been installed three months ago.

DIARY OF EVENTS : THE ACCOUNTS DEPARTMENT OVER THE PAST YEAR

March/April 2002

The company's financial year end was 31 March 2002. The months of March and April were, therefore, characterised by the usual peak in workload for any accounts department at this time of the year. In several areas specific problems in meeting the year end closure routines were experienced.

Mohamed Singh faced considerable problems this month. In his capacity as credit controller (with a brief to reduce year end debts outstanding) he was fully occupied chasing up debtors during the month. This prevented him from keeping up with his work in his other role as sales ledger clerk. By the end of the month Mohamed had only completed the postings for a small amount of the transaction entries affecting the sales ledger, and was working over 60 hours a week (with paid overtime) to try and catch up. Only Sue Moran was sufficiently experienced in operating the sales ledger to be able to provide any meaningful help, but this was however, severely limited because as usual at the year end Sue had enough work of her own to get through. Also she was three years out of practice in working in this area.

Sharon Evans also had great difficulties in meeting the required year end deadlines. During the year Sharon is usually extremely busy during the week of the month-end period, but has relatively little to do during the rest of the month. She knows that the year end period in particular is going to stretch her to the limit, and always tries to get well ahead with her work on direct general ledger postings, the cash book and petty cash so that she can concentrate on producing the trial balance. Since, however, both the sales ledger and the purchase ledger were closed off later than scheduled Sharon, in turn, was unable to complete balancing the trial balance until nearly two weeks after the set date.

The payroll system (that is the system in use at this time, which was subsequently replaced in early January 2003) had been causing problems for quite some time. David Watts, who was the payroll clerk at this time, reported problems caused by its extreme slow running during the month. As well as 31 March being the company's financial year end, the UK tax year ends on 5 April. This makes this an extremely busy time for the payroll clerk, since he was having to complete the normal payroll routines, he has also to ensure that the payroll closure ties in with DEL's internal year end timetable, and then produce the various forms and certificates required by the Inland Revenue. Like Mohamed and Sharon, David was also behind schedule (in this case by four days) in terms of the DEL year end timetable.

These delays in finalising the transaction accounting meant that Elaine Candler, who always personally produces the statutory accounts, had to cancel or delay several important scheduled meetings with outside third parties in order to work full time on the statutory accounts. In particular, she and the managing director had to postpone a meeting with the company's bankers, which had been set to review the financial year 2001/02 accounts. This meeting was important because the company, in addition to renewing its annual overdraft facility was looking to raise a new £250,000 five year term loan to finance a replacement item of machinery.

The only element of light relief in the accounts department this month was a postcard from David Browne, costing technician, telling his colleagues that he was not really enjoying his annual skiing holiday because of the poor covering of snow this year. He did, however, report that the off piste activities were fine.

May 2002

In contrast to the traumas of the past two months, this was a fairly quiet and uneventful month. Very little was seen of the finance director as she spent virtually the whole period off site, either with the company's auditors or in meetings with various banks.

William Whitelow largely concerned himself with reviewing outstanding supplier payments. As is normal practice at DEL, creditors are not generally paid the month before the full year and half year ends, but are then paid in the first two weeks of the following month. Since the company only operates with a relatively small number of suppliers, it is usually possible for Sue Moran, the purchase ledger clerk, to ring them and advise that their payments will be a few weeks late. Most suppliers accept that this tends to be standard business practice, and have no real problem with it. William, however, felt that a full review of the purchase ledger, and in particular of outstanding balances, would be a useful supervisory exercise.

As a result of the problems in failing to meet the year end calendar, Tony Bush was instructed by Elaine Candler to undertake a work re-scheduling and training review. Firstly, Tony was asked to carry out a systematic review of the competencies of the five members of the accounts department (excluding William Whitelow), to recommend what their training needs are and to advise Elaine of the type of training that should be provided. Secondly, he was to recommend ways of re-scheduling the work of the department in order to make the best possible use of both the people working in it and of the systems operated by it.

June 2002

Elaine Candler announced to the staff that the five year term loan for the new machinery had now finally been agreed, but with a different bank than the company's regular bankers.

A major problem mid-month was a power cut, due to fallen electricity cables, which lasted for nearly two days. Although the company does have a standby generator this is only sufficient to power the whole of the factory and offices for up to four hours. The normal practice in the accounts department is to back up all systems at the close of business each day. However, since the power failure occurred in the late afternoon, this meant that all that day's work on all the ledgers, the costing system and the payroll was lost. During the following day the accounts staff could do very little other than basic manual clerical work, and when it became clear that the power would not be restored until late evening the managing director took the decision to close the entire factory and offices for the rest of the day on health and safety grounds.

By the month end the accounts department had managed to effectively catch up their lost work by working a large number of extra hours, as paid overtime. It was generally felt by the staff that their being individually absent for a day or so was never a real problem, except at the year end and half year ends. This is because there is usually sufficient slack in the system to allow for this. However, their being all effectively unable to work for two days did cause great difficulties because of the integrated nature of the transaction accounting system.

July 2002

Tony Bush reported back on the results of the work re-scheduling and training review, and it was agreed that his recommendations would be implemented during the remainder of this financial year.

The old payroll system (that is in use at this time) has, as previously recorded been causing problems for quite some time. This month David Watts, the payroll clerk at this time, reported to William Whitelow that these regular problems of slow running and occasional crashes were continuing to get steadily worse as each month went by.

This system had been installed when the company and its accounts department were first set up, as a stand-alone system running on spreadsheets on a PC. David Watts felt that, whilst this was alright for dealing with the 50 or so people employed at that time, it could no longer cope now that there were over 200 employees.

Since DEL does not have a personnel or HRM officer the personnel records are, by default, manually maintained by the payroll clerk. David and William both agreed that maintaining these manual personnel record cards for the steadily increasing number of employees was getting too overwhelming, and was causing David to duplicate work that he had already done for the payroll system.

August 2002

Tony Bush spent the first two weeks of this month sitting in with David Watts, with the two of them noting which problems occurred on the payroll system during which specific operations. At the end of this review, both had reached the following conclusions. Firstly, that although the existing system could be updated and amended it would not make financial sense to do so, and it would be better to buy in a proprietary payroll software package. Secondly, it would make sense to acquire such a package that also integrated into it a personnel database that could to a large extent be maintained by the same entries as would need to be made for the payroll.

As usual, during August, there were problems caused by staff holidays. Although some aspects of the accounts department's work can be left for a couple of weeks, other, relating to the transaction accounting, always cause difficulties when they are not done on a day by day basis.

For example, no invoices were raised during the second and third weeks of the month because Mohamed Singh was on holiday.

September 2002

It was decided in principle by Elaine Candler that the company would invest in a new integrated payroll and personnel database software package. William Whitelow, David Watts and Tony Bush are to form a steering group to produce a detailed specification of exactly what DEL requires. Then they need to look at the available packages that meet this specification and finally make a cost recommendation to the finance director. Since Tony and David had already started looking at suitable packages it was expected that the three would be able to make a recommendation within the next month or so.

October 2002

Three members of the accounts department staff undertook some form of training this month. These were Sharon Evans, Sue Moran and Mohamed Singh. Training had also been organised for David Browne, but unfortunately David missed it due to being away sick on the relevant three days.

November 2002

The steering committee for the new integrated payroll and personnel database duly reported back, and the selected package was ordered with a scheduled installation date from the software company of the first week in January 2003.

December 2002

Richard West, the managing director, has spent three days this week on a CIMA Master Course on fraud.

January 2003

The new integrated payroll and personnel database was installed on time, and David Watts was due to begin a training programme on it when he announced that he was resigning, having found a better paid position elsewhere. A temp, familiar with the new system, was brought in to cover the payroll whilst a replacement for David was found. All work on maintaining the personnel records was put on hold. William Whitelow undertook to dual run the old system for the next two months' payroll runs as an added test of the new system.

February 2003

David Watts left the company this month, and Rachel Frey, a 22 year old history graduate from Central Polytechnic University, replaced him. The software company who provided DEL with the new payroll and personnel database package provided Rachel with an in-house three day intensive training course on the system.

Product costing was unable to be undertaken for two weeks due to the absence due to sickness of David Browne, the costing technician. Normally David is able to plan his work well in advance to cover his work before going away on holiday etc., but this unexpected sick leave obviously prevented him from doing this. Unfortunately, no other member of staff had the detailed knowledge of the company's products to be able to stand in for David.

March 2003

There were various problems with the new payroll system, and Rachel Frey is getting very worried about coping with the end of tax year P60's, P11D's and so on. In particular, the changes to NIC contribution levels, announced by the Chancellor of the Exchequer in last year's autumn statement, will require immediate updates to this part of the system.

During the month Tony Bush interviewed all members of the accounts department in order to formally report back to the finance director on the update from the work re-scheduling and training review.

Appendix 2 contains the notes of a conversation from the meeting between Tony Bush and Mohamed Singh held on 31 March 2003.

APPENDIX 1

Delmar Electronics Limited: Profit & Loss account for year ended 31/3/03

	2002	2001
	£000	£000
Sales	20,152	18,564
Operating profit	1,364	1,226
Exceptional gain	327	
Net interest payable	(560)	(617)
Currency exchange gain/ (loss)	(415)	(306)
Profit on ordinary activities before tax	716	303
Taxation on profit on ordinary activities	(167)	(68)
Profit on ordinary activities after tax	549	235
Dividends	(183)	(78)
Profit retained for the year	366	157

Delmar Electronics Limited: Balance Sheet as at 31/3/03

	2002	2001
	£000	£000
Fixed assets		
Intangible assets	312	264
Tangible assets	4,556	4,218
	4,868	4,482
Current assets		
Stocks	2,668	2,482
Debtors	5,846	4,127
Cash	361	103
	8,875	6,712
Creditors: amounts falling due within one year	(2,578)	(2,256)
Net current assets	6,297	4,456
Total assets less current liabilities	11,165	8,938
Creditors: amounts falling due after one year	(8,040)	(8,225)
Net assets	3,125	713

APPENDIX 2

Notes of a conversation from the meeting between Tony Bush and Mohamed Singh held on 31/3/2003.

Tony:	Hello Mohamed. As you know I'm interviewing all staff in order to monitor how the changes are going from the work re-scheduling and training review.
Mohamed:	Erm….. right….ok.
Tony:	So how is it going?
Mohamed:	Tony, I've been wanting to talk with you anyway because I erm….. I think we've got a major problem with the way that the purchasing system is being operated.
Tony:	William is your line manager. Have you talked to him about this?
Mohamed:	Erm well yes I would have done – but the thing is I think that whatever is going on he's well sort of involved in it. I'm also a bit nervous about bringing this up with Elaine – I don't want to make a complete fool of myself if I'm wrong. In any event, as you know, she's in hospital recovering from surgery this week.
Tony:	This sounds rather serious, Mohamed. What do you mean?
Mohamed:	You'll remember, of course, that a few months ago you were asked to advise on a work re-scheduling and training review, and that – as part of this – Sue Moran and myself were trained to cover each others work…..
Tony:	Of course I remember….
Mohamed:	Well the thing is whenever I do swap with or cover for Sue, and I've done this perhaps twenty times now, I've never seen any invoices or purchase orders or dealt with any paperwork at all for one of our suppliers – a company called Raymond Briggs Ltd. We've only got around 30 creditors and so it seems odd that this one never comes through on my days on the purchase ledger.
Tony:	Go on…..
Mohamed:	Erm well….. I've looked into the company's records on the purchase ledger, and it seems that we've dealt with them for the past 3 years, but apart from this there's very little information on the system. Far less than for most of our suppliers in fact.
	I then went to see George Stewart about Briggs Ltd. and he immediately clammed up. The next morning I saw him in William Whitelow's office – which is also odd because in all the time I've worked here I can't recall seeing George in the accounts department at all.
Tony:	Has this supplier ever been paid whilst you've been working on the purchase ledger?
Mohamed:	I thought you might ask me that! The answer is no. I've checked back and every payment has been made while Sue Moran has been working on the purchase ledger.
Tony:	Leave this with me – I'll get back to you on it later today.

Candidate Project briefing

BRIEFING FOR A PROJECT REPORT ON THE DELMAR CASE STUDY

Candidates who do not have the opportunity to undertake some form of work-based project are able to provide evidence of competence in this unit by writing a project report based on the material in the Case Study.* The total length of the report should not exceed 4,000 words.

* Publisher's note:

AAT have now indicated that this Case Study is <u>not</u> to be used as a live Simulation.

Candidates should write a report, which demonstrates their underpinning **knowledge and understanding** of:

The Business environment

1   External regulations affecting accounting practices

2   Common types of fraud

3   The implications of fraud

Management techniques

4   Methods of work planning and scheduling

5   Personal time management techniques

6   Methods of measuring cost-effectiveness

7   Methods of fraud detection within accounting systems

8   Techniques for influencing and negotiating with decision makers and resource holders

Management principles and theory

9   Principles of supervision and delegation

10   Principles of creating effective inter-personal relationships, team building and staff motivation

The organisation

11   The impact on an accounting system of organisational structure, Management Information Systems, administrative systems and procedures and the nature of its business transactions

12   The organisation's business and its relationships with external stakeholders

13   The purpose, structure and organisation of the accounting system and its inter-relation with other internal functions

14   The control of resources by individuals within the organisation

This can be demonstrated by writing a project report of up to 4,000 words, addressed to Elaine Candler – the finance director, which covers the following:

■ **The co-ordination of work activities within DEL's accounting environment**

This candidate must demonstrate his/her ability to plan and co-ordinate DEL's accounts department's work activities effectively. Including setting and monitoring realistic objectives, targets and deadlines and managing people so that these can be met. In addition the candidate needs to show that he/she can develop contingency plans to deal with a range of problems that may detract from the organisation meeting those objectives, targets and deadlines.

■ **Identification of opportunities to improve the effectiveness of DEL's accounting system**

The Candidate must demonstrate his/her ability to identify weaknesses in DEL's accounting system, and making recommendations to rectify these; to consider the impact that these would have on the organisation; to update the system to comply for example with legislative changes; and to subsequently check that the post-change output is now correct.

The project report should be both holistic and strategic in nature. That is, the candidate should report on each of the detailed areas listed below, and then bring these together in an integrated way so that the overall position can be seen. From this he/she should then identify perhaps four to six major issues, which are of strategic importance to DEL.

In detail the project should include:

■ How the candidate would plan and monitor work routines to meet DEL's organisational time schedules and to make the best use of both their human and physical resources (Performance Criterion A [PC A]). Planning and scheduling this project report for completion to standard and on time will also provide evidence towards (PC A).

■ The systematic review of staff competencies and training needs, together with details of the training actually arranged (PC B).

■ Contingency planning for possible emergencies, (eg computer system not being fully functional, staff absences, and changes in work patterns and demands) (PC C).

■ How the candidate would communicate work methods and schedules to colleagues so that they have understood what is expected of them (PC D).

■ How the candidate would monitor work activities closely against quality standards to ensure they are being met (PC E).

■ How the candidate would co-ordinate work activities effectively against work plans and contingency plans (PC F).

■ How the candidate would encourage colleagues to report promptly, issues beyond their authority and expertise. How he/she would resolve these where possible (PC G), or otherwise refer such issues to the appropriate person to resolve them (PC H).

■ A situation analysis of the accounting system under scrutiny (eg a SWOT analysis), which will generate evidence towards Performance Criteria A & B.

■ Evidence of resulting recommendations made to the appropriate people in a clear understandable format and supported by a clear rationale. This will generate evidence towards PCs D & E. All assumptions made should be clearly listed.

■ Evidence of research, pointing towards potential areas of fraud within DEL's accounting system (eg teeming and lading, fictitious employees or suppliers). Research into appropriate fraud risk standards will generate evidence for PC B. Candidates are advised to use some form of matrix approach towards grading the various elements of risk.

■ How the candidate would undertake a regular view of methods of operating, providing evidence for PC C.

■ How the candidate would update the system in accordance with both internal factors (eg changes in the organisational structure, responses to customer surveys) and external factors (eg changes in company law, VAT rates, FRS's) that require such updates to be made. This provides evidence for PC F – SWOT and PEST analyses respectively would be useful here.

Any of the above evidence that does not sit naturally within the project report should be included as additional evidence in the appendices to it. If the listed Performance Criteria and Underpinning Knowledge and Understanding have NOT been addressed sufficiently by the project content documented, then assessor questioning MUST be employed to address any gaps.

ALL Performance Criteria and Underpinning Knowledge and Understanding must be evidenced.

Notes for Assessors – Delmar Project Report

NOTE TO ASSESSORS

The project report should be both holistic and strategic in nature. That is, the candidate should have reported on each of the detailed areas listed in the briefing notes for candidates. He/she should then bring these together in an integrated way so that the overall position can be seen. From this he/she should then identify perhaps four to six major issues, which are of strategic importance to DEL.

ASSESSMENT CRITERIA

The solutions suggested here are indicative only. In some cases, it is likely that candidates will produce valid alternative answers, perhaps from a completely different paradigmal perspective. Assessors should, therefore, look for underpinning knowledge, understanding of the key issues in the simulation and for reasonable method and process.

IT IS NOT THE AAT's INTENTION TO PRODUCE INDICATIVE SOLUTIONS FOR FUTURE CASE STUDIES. THESE HAVE BEEN PRODUCED FOR THIS INITIAL CASE STUDY ONLY TO GIVE ASSESSORS A BENCHMARK AGAINST WHICH TO ASSESS FUTURE PROJECTS.

PLANNING & MONITORING WORK ROUTINES

Here the key principle is that of separation of duties by some over-riding need (in this case the month end timetable) rather than by function (eg sales ledger work). Candidates could separate work by other well argued, valid means. Providing they demonstrate that their proposals optimise the use and time of the available personnel.

STAFF COMPETENCIES & TRAINING NEEDS REVIEW

The essential issue here is that before the review, all members of the accounts department can only work with their own individual part of the system, and also need to be trained so that they can work with at least one other part. The actual proposals as to who does what are fairly arbitrary, (based on employees' past experience), and candidates will doubtless produce many other viable suggestions.

CONTINGENCY PLANNING

Candidates should be able to explain what is meant by contingency planning and should be able to make some reasonable suggestions to cover both staff absences and computer system failure.

SITUATION ANALYSIS OF THE ACCOUNTING SYSTEM

Candidates at this level can be expected to produce a comprehensive, professional SWOT analysis. They should be able to conclude that in general the sales system works effectively, the payroll system needs some improvement and the purchases system is fundamentally weak. The detailed comments need not necessarily be as per those in the suggested solution.

The purchases and supplier payments systems and procedures must be identified as the weakest individual part. Candidates should be able to make recommendations, which relate to the purchase ledger system, ordering or receipt of goods.

POTENTIAL AREAS OF FRAUD

The aim of this part of the assessment is to give candidates the opportunity to apply their underpinning knowledge to a specific context. Assessors should expect that the weaker candidates, relying on route learning, are likely to experience difficulty here.

All candidates should be able to identify perhaps four areas at risk from fraud in the purchases and supplier payments system.

They should also be able to explain how these risks arise.

ENCOURAGING COLLEAGUES TO REPORT ISSUES & RESOLVING OR REFERRING THEM

This section of the standards is extremely difficult to assess (whether by work-based project or by case study simulation). Due to the subjectivity implicit in the performance criteria here, assessors should expect a variety of different approaches. Again, look for reasoned arguments and underpinning knowledge of the issues involved, rather than precise answers as per the indicative solution.

REVIEW OF METHODS OF OPERATING/UPDATES TO THE SYSTEM & RESULTING RECOMMENDATIONS

Candidates can demonstrate their competence in these areas in a variety of ways by using the material in the Case Study. One obvious way is to include in the report a recommendation to the board for a series of control checks that should be introduced over the purchase and supplier payments system.

Suggested Report Extracts

INDICATIVE REPORT EXTRACTS COVERING THE MAIN STRATEGIC ISSUES FROM THE CASE STUDY

To: Elaine Candler   **From**: Tony Bush

Training needs review identifying the competencies and training requirements of each of the five members of the accounts department.

The starting point should be to establish what skills, knowledge and competencies DEL requires its accounts staff to have, and then decide whether these can be met internally or whether we need to recruit externally. I would suggest that the training required ensures that all members of staff become skilled and competent to operate at least two parts of the accounting system.

Considering each individual employee:

Sharon Evans, General Ledger Clerk

Sharon seems somewhat under-employed, in that other members of staff enter the sales and purchase figures into the GL – leaving Sharon only the direct entries (such as purchases of fixed assets) to make. In addition Sharon maintains the cashbook and petty cash and does the bank reconciliations. The obvious area for Sharon to be trained in seems to be the payroll & personnel database. Since she has previously worked in HR she may well be interested and well suited to this work. This would also relieve the pressure on Rachel Frey, who is both a young and inexperienced member of staff but seems however to have a very heavy workload.

Sue Moran, Purchase Ledger Clerk

Since Sue is already familiar with DEL's sales ledger system, it would make sense from the company's point of view to give her refresher training in this area, so that she could cover for Mohamed Singh. Sue has started taking AAT qualifications, and to support her in this, DEL should also offer her training in a further new area of the accounts system – perhaps the GL or costing system.

Mohamed Singh, Sales Ledger Clerk and Credit Controller

Mohamed's previous job was as a purchase ledger clerk with another electronics company. Logically from DEL's point of view, he should be trained to operate the purchase ledger. Apart from the added flexibility, the accounts department may benefit from Mohamed being able to recommend changes to DEL purchase ledger practices, based on his experience at Withern Electronics Ltd. Longer term, the company should seek to meet Mohamed's expressed interest in gaining either accounting or credit control qualifications.

David Browne, Costing Technician

From the information provided, David is the only employee who apparently has experience in costing the company's products. This places DEL in an exposed situation because, unlike maintaining the ledgers, costing requires detailed knowledge of the company's products. Another member of staff needs to be trained in this area as a matter of urgency. Based on David's previous background in credit control, it would be logical to train him in DEL's credit control procedures. David's reluctance to undertake training and development needs to be investigated and resolved.

Rachel Frey, Payroll & Personnel Database Clerk

As well as being the newest and youngest member of staff, Rachel is also working on by far the newest part of the system and therefore, the part most likely to experience problems. To cope with this she has only been given three days intensive training. Rachel should be given at least a further period of update training by the software company who sold DEL the system. Beyond this, her own development needs should be discussed with her and further training/development arranged.

Advice on how, after the training needs have been met, work activities could be rescheduled to optimise the use and time of the available accounts department personnel.

The fundamental aim of the training needs analysis was to multi-skill the accounts department staff. Previously they could each only effectively do their own specific job but after training they are able to undertake at least one other function. However, to maintain and develop their new skills, staff should have their work rescheduled so that they *regularly and as a matter of course* work in this other function, otherwise the training is likely to be forgotten.

The work of the department could be viewed and organised in several different ways. At present it is viewed as a series of disparate functional activities (sales ledger, payroll etc). Another way of scheduling work would be to divide it into what needs to be done according to the month-end timetable and what does not. In the first category would fall activities such as closing the ledgers, extracting the trial balance and running the monthly payroll. In the second category would fall activities such as updating customer, supplier and personnel records and costing products.

As presently organised, the month-end routines severely affect some members of staff (such as Sharon Evans), whilst others (such as David Browne) are not really affected at all. This makes poor use of resources and time when considered from the viewpoint of the department as a whole.

An effective way, therefore, of rescheduling the workload would be by following the two principles:

- Staff all undertaking work in two areas.

- Activities being spread amongst staff in order to divide them between those crucial month-end routines and those, which are not.

Obviously these two principles may conflict at times and much more information would be needed to put this properly into practice. However, as an example David Browne (once trained in DEL's credit control practices) could leave most of his costing work to the final week of the month and chase up debtors. This would both allow Mohamed Singh to concentrate all his energies on the month-end sales ledger routines, and hopefully result in a lower figure of month-end debtors and higher cash at bank.

Explanation of the term "contingency planning", and a contingency plan, after the training needs review and work activity rescheduling has been implemented.

Contingency planning

Contingency planning involves assessing, and subsequently planning how best to manage, unplanned events, which may occur from time to time. In practical terms these are events where there is both a reasonable probability of them happening AND that the impact of them actually happening would be significant for the business. For example, the likelihood of an aircraft crashing directly on DEL's premises is not of a high order of probability and, although its effect on the business would be very significant, it would not normally be included in a contingency plan. This type of event is often covered by "shock event planning", and would be covered by risk transference, which usually means insurance. On the other hand, although there is a high probability that the accounts department might run out of paperclips the effect on the business of this happening would not be significant, so this event too would not form part of a contingency plan.

Staff absences

A contingency plan for staff absences is fairly straightforward since it largely emanates from the outcome of the training needs review and have the work rescheduling exercise.

Since all staff are now able to operate at least two parts of the accounting system, the absence of any one employee can be readily covered by his/her "shadow". For example, since both Sue Moran and Mohamed Singh can run both the purchases and sales ledgers, Sue can, at least for a limited period, run both ledgers in Mohamed's absence, and vice versa.

Problems arise where more than one employee is absent at the same time and/or where an employee is absent near the month-end (or worse still half year or year end) period.

Where more than one employee is absent, or an employee is absent at a critical period end, it will be necessary to utilise additional resources from outside the transaction accounting staff. Essentially, this means either:

■ using myself, David Browne or even William Whitelow because the work that we do has, in general, less immediate impact on the business if it is left until later.

■ using outside contract agency staff.

Failure of the company's computer system

In many ways this is far more difficult to plan for than staff absences because there is a larger number of events and variables, which could cause a failure of the computer system.

An effective contingency plan for the failure of computer systems needs to consider both a partial failure (affecting one part of the system only) and a total failure (affecting all parts of the system). A failure affecting more than one part of the system, but not the total system can probably for most practical purposes be considered to have the same implications as a total failure.

A partial failure could, for example, be caused by the failure of an individual element of the system such as the payroll & personnel database or the costing system being corrupted by a virus. Since these two systems are stand alone and not integrated with any other part of the system, the impact of this should be contained to those parts directly affected only.

A total failure could, for example, be caused by a computer virus destroying or corrupting all the files on the hard disk of the main integrated financial accounting system, or by a power cut.

All possible causes of a partial failure should, as far as possible, be identified and their probabilities and effects on the business assessed. For example, a failure of the costing system might cause the loss of a day or so's work by David Browne before the fault can be rectified. The cost of this can be usefully employed elsewhere in the department. Those partial failures that meet the definition for inclusion in contingency planning given above should be formally planned for.

Costs of a total system failure are more difficult to estimate, but an attempt should be made in general terms to do so.

Once risks have been identified and assessed, the next step is to manage them. This could include any combination of the following contingencies:

- Of paramount importance is the regular back up of data and software, so that in the event of failure it is only the hardware which needs to be supplied. If this is not undertaken the rest of the contingency plan, however good, is doomed to failure.

- Spreading computer facilities over more than one site or system, so that work can be transferred from the lost site or system. Since all DEL's systems stand alone apart from the main financial accounting system, this is the part of the system most in need of "distributed support".

- Subscribing to a facilities management service, which would allow DEL to buy into a shared standby computer service.

The effectiveness of DEL's business & accounting practices and policies

Our business & accounting practices and policies include purchases & supplier payments, sales & customer receipts, and payroll & personnel database administration. These are supported by the relevant parts of our accounting system, ie the general ledger, purchase ledger, sales ledger, credit control, costing, payroll & the personnel database. To identify which parts are good/satisfactory and which parts need improvement, I have prepared a SWOT analysis:

SWOT ANALYSIS

STRENGTHS

Purchases & supplier payments:

- The company buyer, George Stewart, and the purchase ledger clerk are both experienced at their jobs, having been in these positions for four and three years respectively.

- The benefits of the "partnership sourcing" scheme, are the reduced admin. costs and long-term stability in terms of supplies, prices and quality.

Sales & customer receipts:

- Overall, this part of the system works very effectively.

- Again, the sales ledger clerk, Mohamed Singh, has three years experience at doing this job.

- The system for giving open credit, and increasing credit limits is effective. A three month trial period should be more than sufficient for DEL to both get familiar with the customer and to thoroughly credit check them. The involvement of the sales force in this process should result in useful market knowledge based information being available. Approval for credit limits and changes to them are made at the most senior level, by either the FD or MD.

- Sales invoices and cheques are both banked daily.

- Different people carry out the banking & accounting postings (Mohamed Singh) and the bank reconciliation (Sharon Evans).

- The aged debtors listing is used effectively with a two tier level of review, and with the involvement of the relevant directors at an appropriate time.

Payroll & personnel records:

- The use of BACS to pay all monthly employees and 80% of those paid hourly.

- The use of an integrated payroll and personnel database should lead to increased efficiency, as compared to two individual system.

WEAKNESSES

Purchases & supplier payments:

- This is by far the weakest part of the overall system, and is potentially open to fraud.

- Three employees control virtually the entire process (George Stewart, Sue Moran & William Whitelow). George & William were instrumental in introducing the present system, and George & Sue are father and daughter. The only third party checks against potential fraud are the final second signatures on the cheque or BACS run. Even these are rarely done by the FD, but by one of the other directors, who will have little time to do any independent checks.

Sales & customer receipts:

■ None apparent.

Payroll & personnel records:

■ The 20% of the hourly paid payroll paid in cash results in a disproportionate amount of work, cost and the risk of theft.

■ The payroll & personnel records clerk, Rachel Frey, is both new to the company and not properly trained on the system.

■ The system itself is new, but does not seem to be being monitored for weaknesses or errors.

OPPORTUNITIES

Purchases & supplier payments:

■ Since the present policy has been in place for three years, and the existing 30 suppliers are on two to three year contracts, there is now an opportunity to get NEW suppliers to tender for the next cycle of contracts. This would not necessarily increase the overall number of suppliers, but would allow fresh blood into the tendering system. It would also reduce the risk of fraud through collusion between an existing long-standing supplier and the buyer (plus the two other DEL employees involved).

Sales & customer receipts:

■ The three month cash with order basis should be reviewed for any evidence that this is causing DEL to lose business. Is the policy applied across the board, eg to plc's?

■ 84% (210/240) of DEL's customers contribute only 20% of the profit. A pareto-type customer profitability analysis should be carried out to identify any customers who are unprofitable or whether their profitability is too low for the support they require. An ABC system would help here.

Payroll & personnel records:

■ The existing cash paid employees should be given an incentive to move to a BACS payment system, and all the new employees should be automatically paid in this way.

■ Rachel Frey needs more comprehensive training, as per task 1 above.

■ Is the personnel database being used to its maximum extent? Given Rachel's lack of training and the fact that both she and the system are new, it is likely that only the key payroll aspects are being properly used.

THREATS

Purchases & supplier payments:

- This part of the system is at threat from fraud. It would be possible for the company buyer to collude with one or more of DEL's long-standing suppliers to eg agree higher than arms length prices, or to sign off goods not actually received etc. The "back hander" from the supplier would then be shared with the two other DEL employees who control the system.

- Apart from fraud, there is a danger of complacency on the part of the suppliers, who may see themselves in a cosy relationship with DEL and feel able to creep up prices because of the lack of competition. These type of arrangements must be subject to regular audit by a senior member of DEL – probably Elaine Candler.

Sales & customer receipts:

- None apparent.

Payroll & personnel records:

- The cash payments to employees are at risk of theft.

The weakest individual part

From the SWOT analysis it is clear that the purchases and supplier payments system is by far the weakest individual part of the whole.

Detailed recommendations (two from the following) for its improvement include:

- The establishment of a Purchase Ledger Control account, maintained and periodically checked against the purchase ledger by another member of staff, probably the GL clerk.

- A better separation of duties between those employees who are receiving goods, maintaining the purchase ledger, authorising invoices, checking suppliers' statements to the purchase ledger account and running payment routines.

- Reviewing the financial stability checks currently carried out by Sue Moran. Perhaps the responsibilities could be rescheduled so that the sales ledger clerk can check out both potential customers AND suppliers.

- All cheques and BACS payments should be properly reviewed before they receive a director's second signature. Ideally the FD should undertake this, but in her absence another specified director who can make time available should deputise. An alternative would be for two directors (and not the company accountant) to sign off all payments to suppliers.

Identification of the risks of fraud in the weakest individual part of DEL's accounting systems.

As identified earlier, the purchase and supplier payment system is the weakest element of our systems, and the potential for fraud has already been outlined in general terms.

A risk management group (RMG) should be established to review the risks, including those of fraud, in the purchase and supplier payments system. The board of directors needs to decide on the level of risk that DEL is prepared to accept. Once this has been done the RMG should understand and assess the scale of risks in this part of the system, prioritise these by the scale of their possible impact and probability of occurring, and then go on to develop a risk management strategy.

In considering the possible composition of this group, DEL should look for individuals with expertise in the company's systems and procedures, a basic knowledge of fraud, and the knowledge and authority to introduce changes to procedures and new controls. The obvious person to chair the RMG is the finance director, Elaine Candler. I would also recommend that myself, as accounting systems technician, and William Whitelow, company accountant, are part of the group. It would also be of benefit to have at least one non-finance/accounting individual on the group in order to provide a different perspective on the issues. One of the other directors or a manager from a different area would be appropriate.

Risk Analysis of potential fraud in the purchases and supplier payments system			
Details of Risk	*Employees*	*Third Parties*	*Collusion by*
Scoping of Contract	DEL buyer		Buyer & Suppliers
Favourable contract terms & conditions	DEL buyer		Buyer & Suppliers
Changing evaluation Criteria	DEL buyer		Buyer & Suppliers
Changing contract terms & conditions	DEL buyer		Company accountant
False invoices and authorisations	DEL buyer	Suppliers	Purchase Ledger clerk
Inflated Pricing	DEL buyer	Suppliers	
Paying fictitious or controlled suppliers	DEL buyer		Purchase Ledger clerk Company accountant

How these risks arise

Scoping of the contract:

Contract specifications are written so as to favour one particular buyer, eg by specifying very tight and specific attributes, which only one supplier's product can meet.

Favourable contract terms & conditions:

The terms of the contract are altered in order to either exclude other companies from tendering or to accommodate the requirements of the favoured supplier.

Changing evaluation criteria:

The original criteria for deciding who gets a contract are subsequently changed, i.e. after all the tendering has been done, must ensure that the favoured supplier gains the contract.

Changing contract terms and conditions:

After the contract has been awarded to the favoured supplier, the terms and conditions are altered in his favour.

False invoices or authorisations:

The favoured supplier colludes with the buyer to produce invoices for goods not supplied. This would probably require the collusion of the purchase ledger clerk.

Inflated pricing:

The favoured supplier increases the prices of goods supplied, and the buyer approves these artificially inflated prices.

Paying fictitious or controlled suppliers:

The buyer produces false invoices from a fictitious supplier or one controlled by himself.

Assessment of risk in terms of likelihood of occurrence and potential damage to the business.					
Area of Risk	Probability	Impact	Controls	Net likely impact	Action
Scoping of contract	High	High	Low	High	Priority
Favourable contract Terms & conditions	High	High	Low	High	Priority
Changing evaluation Criteria	High	High	Low	High	Priority
Changing contract Terms & conditions	High	Medium	Low	Medium	Second Order priority
False invoices and authorisations	Medium	High	Low	Medium	Second Order priority
Inflated Pricing	High	High	Low	High	Priority
Paying fictitious or controlled suppliers	Low	High	Low	Medium	Second Order priority

The company should be very concerned by the high net impact on the business arising from several areas at risk. A common element of this is the low level of controls across every area of this part of the system. The only reason that probabilities can be considered low or medium in two areas is the need for collusion between two or more DEL employees.

Encouraging colleagues to report issues and resolving or referring these

Referring to the notes of the conversation from a confidential meeting between myself and Mohamed Singh (see Appendix 2) and to the further consideration of fraud risk.

Preliminary investigations and checks, if any, I would personally undertake in this matter:

Mohamed Singh has provided *prima facie* evidence of fraud only, i.e. based on first impressions there appears to be fraud or malpractice in the purchases & supplier payment procedures. This is not the same as *substantiated* evidence, which would only be provided by undertaking investigations and checks.

Before taking any further action myself, or referring the matter to higher management, it would be appropriate to undertake at least some preliminary investigations, as at the moment the only "evidence" is Mohamed's verbal statement. Furthermore, he himself has not been prepared to proactively "whistleblow", but has only raised the issue as part of a scheduled systems review interview. Finally, in the finance director's absence (through hospitalisation) and with the company accountant's possible involvement in the suspected fraud I am really the only individual with the skills and knowledge to at least start preliminary investigations.

That said, my investigations should be severely restricted to the minimum level needed to provide at least some hard evidence. Essentially, this means checking the system only, and not for both legal and practical reasons (i.e. alerting the suspects) and not getting involved with interviewing any other members of staff.

Preliminary investigations and checks would therefore, be restricted to unobtrusively finding out as much as possible about Raymond Briggs Ltd. This would include:

- Interrogating the computer system in order to obtain a full record of the transaction history between DEL and Briggs. Details of all purchase orders, goods received notes; invoices, credit/debit notes and payments should be obtained.

- Obtaining a full credit check and, if possible, annual report for Briggs. Amongst other things this would reveal who its directors are and where its registered office is.

- If possible, obtaining copies of all the tendering documentations involving Briggs. This includes contract specifications, contract terms and conditions, the criteria for awarding the contract to this particular supplier; any subsequent changes to the original contract prices etc.

Whether I myself have the authority and expertise to take the matter further or whether I need to refer it to someone else:

As the accounting systems technician it is questionable whether or not I should personally undertake preliminary investigations and checks, or whether I should immediately refer the matter to more senior management. On balance, I believe that the right course of action has been to undertake limited preliminary checks. Once this has been done, I believe that I have reached the limit of my authority and expertise, and assuming there is some hard evidence, I will now refer the matter to higher management. The over-riding point is that I have restricted my investigations to the minimum that it is reasonable for me, in my position, to undertake. Full investigations, including interviewing staff are the responsibility of a formal investigation team, the composition of which will be determined by the directors.

The most appropriate person to refer the matter to:

Although William Whitelow is Mohamed's supervisor, he is also one of the three employees, who are *prima facie* implicated in the potential fraud. It would, therefore, not be appropriate to refer the matter to him. The obvious person to refer the matter to is the finance director, Elaine Candler, or in her absence the matter should be referred to the managing director, Richard West.

Review of methods of operating/updates to the system and resulting recommendations

I would recommend to the board that the following control checks should be introduced over the purchases and supplier payments system:

For purchase orders:

■   All requisition notes for purchases should be authorised by the appropriate departmental manager.

■   All purchase orders should be authorised by the buyer or the appropriate manager, and approval limits should be formally set.

■   Beyond a certain level of expenditure, significant orders, such as for capital expenditure should be approved by the board.

■   All orders should be made on official letter-head purchase orders, and should show the supplier's name, the specification of the goods/services ordered and the agreed price.

■   Purchase orders should be in multipart set format, with copies being retained to provide both an audit trail and a means of resolving queries.

■   Re-order levels should, wherever possible, be set in advance and entered on the requisition note.

For receipt of purchased goods:

■   All goods should be delivered to a designated goods inwards centre only.

■   On arrival at the designated centre goods should be inspected to ensure that they meet the specifications on the supplier's delivery note. Once the quantities and condition of the goods have been agreed, a Goods Received Note (GRN) should be raised and signed by the goods inwards supervisor.

■   The GRN should then be matched up with the purchase order. At this stage the delivery note, the quantity and quality of the physical goods and the purchase order will have been checked against each other and agreed. Suppliers will then be notified of under or over-deliveries.

■   GRN's should be pre-printed with sequential numbers, and periodically checked for completeness by someone other than a goods inwards employee.

Index